*Unpacking Everyday Wisdom:
Stories of Vulnerability, Strength,
and the Human Heart*

Lorie Kleiner Eckert

Chai on Life

Copyright 2025: Lorie Kleiner Eckert. All rights reserved

No part of this book may be reproduced in any form or by electronic means, including information storage and retrieval systems, without written permission from the publisher, except by a reviewer, who may quote passages in a review.

Cover Design: Christine Van Bree
Interior Design: Tracy Copes
Illustrations created on Canva by Lorie Kleiner Eckert.
Author Photo: Lisa Griebling

978-1-61088-669-7 (HC)
978-1-61088-670-3 (PB)
978-1-61088-671-0 (ebook)
978-1-61088-672-7 (ePDF)
978-1-61088-673-4 (Audiobook)

Published by Bancroft Press
"Books that Enlighten"
4527 Glenwood Avenue, La Crescenta, CA 91214
www.bancroftpress.com | (818) 275-3061
Printed in the United States of America

"Chai" is a mystical word in Hebrew.

It is pronounced "high,"

making this book

High on Life —

with a Jewish slant.

CONTENTS

Prelude

Accepting Yourself and Others
- I Am Who I Am..7
- The More I Look for My Mom, the More I Find Her in My Heart 13
- Convincing Myself to Be Courageous...19
- My Stomach Is Flat, but the L Is Silent...25
- Shrunken Heads vs Inflated Ones—In Praise of Praise 27

Life 101 – A Formula for Living
- The Importance of Having a Game Plan 35
- Moving a Little Bit at a Time Toward a Rich Life 39
- Doing Splits at Thanksgiving...45
- Good Enough Is Good Enough..51
- Odd Life Lessons from the Gym 57

Personal Reinvention
- A COVID-19 Correction to My Vision 65
- Reinventing Yourself – A How-To 71

Eureka! I Have Found it: This Is Happiness
- I've Got it Figured Out, This Is What Happiness Is..........................81
- But What About the Fact that Life Is Difficult? 87
- Is Jumping Naked into the Lake the Key to Happiness? 93
- How to Be Rich in Friends...99
- Flipping My Switch...105

Some Odds and Ends to Mention

- Deciphering Hillel Through the Years 113
- In a Billy Joel State of Mind – A Story about Anger and Forgiveness 121
- Is There a Stigma to Getting Psychological Help? I Don't Feel It! 127
- That Time I Needed a Husband 131
- Three Reasons to Write in a Journal 137

Aging

- Being the Patient vs the Visitor in the Emergency Room 145
- Still Young Enough to Have a Crush 151
- My Personal State of the Union Address 155
- Learning from Margot in Life and in Death 163
- Worrying about Field Sobriety Tests and Other Aspects of Aging 169

Can't Help Loving that Family of Mine

- We Are Family 177
- Canned Pink Salmon, Prunes, and Dried Apricots 183
- On Matzah Balls, Legos, and Various Things Between 185
- Influencers Are Everywhere, Not Just on Social Media 191
- Upon Turning Seventy 197

The G Words – Gratitude and God

- 30 Reasons to Be Grateful at My Granddaughter's Soccer Game 205
- Long Story Listener 211
- From God's Lips to My Ears 217
- God Dancing on the Ceiling 221

The Whole Book in Short Form 227
About the Author 231
A Note in Closing from Me.. 235
Notes to Yourself from You.. 236

PRELUDE

Mindset is Important When Looking in a Magic Mirror: A Story for Uncertain Times

A few years ago, my granddaughter and I played together with her Barbies. As we started our play, Cookie gave me one of the dolls and told me to fix its hair. So, I did. I braided the doll's hair into one thick ponytail. Turning it toward her, I asked, "How's this?" Her response was swift, "Horrible!" I chuckled then, but didn't find it so amusing when every time I checked my own hair in the mirror after that, her disparaging word echoed in my head.

Fast forward a couple of years to another grandchild, two-year-old Jude. As his name might suggest, his family and he love the Beatles. Jude's favorite Beatle is John Lennon and he loves to play with the John Lennon glasses I have at my house. Each pair of granny-type-glasses has different colored lenses. The first time we played with them he put on the glasses with blue lenses. I clapped my hands with joy and said, "Let's go look in the mirror and see how handsome you look!" And so, we ran off to look in the mirror. We repeated the process with the pink lenses and the purple ones. He always looked so handsome!

After several days of playing this game, Jude played it a new way. He put on a pair of glasses, marched over to the mirror, and proudly and loudly proclaimed, "Look how handsome I look!"

And guess what? Now when I check my image in that mirror, *his* words are the words I hear as I go from horrible to handsome without changing my makeup, my hairdo, or my clothing style. All that has changed is my mindset.

As we go through our difficult days, remember the magic mirror. Mindset is the key.

I hope you like that story. I wrote it in March 2020 when, because of Covid, life was so uncertain. It's representative of what I have done professionally for the last thirty years as a motivational speaker, author, columnist, and blogger. My M.O. is to tell the stories of my life hoping others can glean life lessons from them. If you like this concept, turn the page! Three dozen stories await you. Some of them have been published previously, and some are new, written just for this book, but all carry life lessons that are worth remembering—lessons such as as this one:

Accepting Yourself and Others

I AM WHO I AM
January 5, 2021

In 1993, when I was in the throes of marital difficulties, my dad said something that remains the kindest, most understanding thing anyone has ever said to me. My now ex-husband and I had separated, and were trying to disrupt our children's lives as little as possible. We each had our own apartment, and we took turns moving back into the family home when it was our week to have custody of the kids.

Dad said he hoped my husband and I got back together again, but even if we did, he thought we should keep my apartment because I am the sort of person who needs lots of quiet time to herself. Given that Dad was a very frugal man and a very traditional thinker, this was radical advice. That he could acknowledge my non-conventional needs and be so accepting of them was my first step on the journey toward accepting...

...Who I am:

I am an indoor-sy person.

Chai on Life

I love my home.
Except to go for a morning walk,
it doesn't occur to me to go outside.
Impacted by long-ago losses in the Holocaust,
I cherish my family,
and try to stay close to them
and to several friends who are like family.
Even having all these loved ones,
I think of myself as a misanthrope,
and say I don't like people.
In truth, I get my feelings hurt easily,
and take things personally,
making it safer not to engage.
I often have a lot to say,
but not everyone is willing to listen.
Thus, I love to write.
I love to read
and often to sew.

LORIE KLEINER ECKERT

I like to putter:
to straighten things up,
to put things away,
to turn lots of little notes into lists.
Then I love to scratch things off the list!
Most days I feel content
and rich in love.
Except when I feel all alone.
About "blue" days, Dad instructed me:
Remember yesterday and tomorrow.
And so, I recall the grandson
who saw me in an animal-print sweater
and asked why I was dressed like a zebra.
It always makes me laugh.
And I recall my
walking partners,
travel partners,
movie partners,

Chai on Life

theater partners,

ice cream partners,

and sitting-at-the-bar partners

and reach out to one of them

to restore my

needing solitude vs.

needing people equilibrium.

That difficult balance beam,

which has always been mine to walk.

So that's who I am.

And it's ok.

Dad said so.

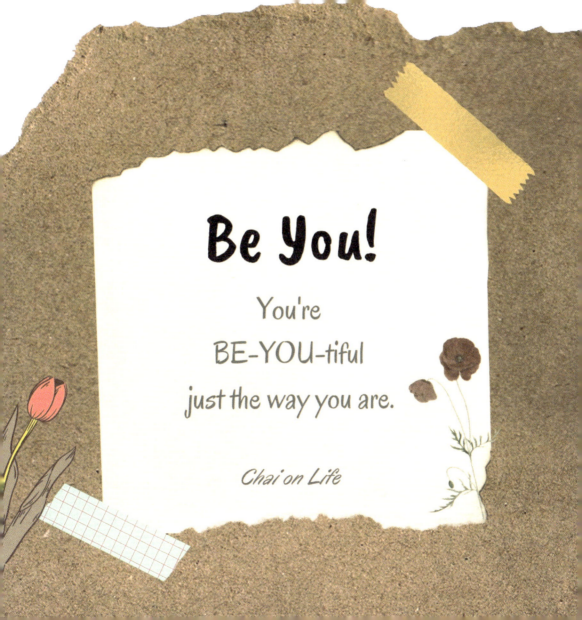

THE MORE I LOOK FOR MY MOM, THE MORE I FIND HER IN MY HEART

January 12, 2021

I remember talking to my mom about my generation of pampered women who were lovingly/mockingly labeled "JAPs"—Jewish American Princesses. She told me that in her generation, it was the Jewish American Prince who was all important.

This being the case, she first served her prince, my Dad, as a stay-at-home wife, and then, in the role of stay-at-home mom, her princess—me (my brother got his fair share of royal treatment too). In Dad's case, he didn't know where to find a water glass in the kitchen because if he wanted a drink, she got it for him. In my case, it was memorable to wash dishes at my aunt's house because I was never asked to wash dishes at home.

None of this seemed to bother my mom. By the same token, none of this seemed to impress those of us who received her many gifts.

Chai on Life

As a teenager, I didn't always get along with her. In fact, I found her quite annoying at times. Her main offense was wearing Merry Mules to walk around the house. They slapped at her heels. They announced her arrival. They made me feel like I was under surveillance. She was ever-present!

But of course, she *was* ever-present. How else could she get the dinners cooked, the lunches packed, the house cleaned, the bills paid, and the laundry washed, ironed, mended, and put away? And how could she get all the dishes washed, because really, who else could/would do them?

Mom wasn't one to complain, to bad-mouth, to get angry. Instead, she let things "roll off her back" and lived by the motto: "If you can't say something nice, don't say anything at all."

Though she had close friends, I doubt she aired any personal grievances with them. I see it now as an honor that she brought her rare complaints to me. It seems that Mom's mother—my Bubbie—made her crazy. Every week, Mom chauffeured her to several grocery stores so Bubbie could get tuna on sale here, and prunes on sale there, and the best price on flour at the third place. All the while, Bubbie complained that none of her kids came to see her, a statement which made Mom, her eldest child, feel invisible.

I did an equally fine job of applying white-out to Mom's many gifts to me. Each time I had a baby, she came from Missouri to whatever state I lived to help out for a full month. (By the way, this is when Dad, who stayed in St. Louis, learned which cupboard held the water glasses.) She was more comfortable doing the laundry, cleaning, and cooking than baby tending, so she did all those tasks while I handled the newborn.

I would love to chalk this up to post-partum insanity, but my response to this amazing gift was to be annoyed with her. Her main offence was she didn't fold bath towels the right way. My first fold is vertical because that's the way it's going to get hung on the towel rack. Her first fold was horizontal, requiring me to—gasp!—refold it before hanging it up.

Yes, indeed, I was a princess, or maybe a five-letter word that starts with B and that my mother would never, ever say.

But here is something that she did say, and indeed, she said it often. When she spoke of my teenage years, she said she was grateful because we got along so well. I always wondered what relationship with what daughter she was talking about. However, I sure hope she felt the same way about our adult relationship. I hope none of my antics clung to her back, giving her not nice things to not say.

Chai on Life

I always thought I'd figure out a way to be a non-perturbable daughter and to have a great relationship with Mom. Unfortunately, time ran out. In 2002, when she was 81-years old, she was diagnosed with lung cancer.

As I sat with her in the hospital, I wanted to say two things that were not said in our home. First, I wanted to call myself a bitch and apologize for the cussing and the bitchiness. And second, I wanted to say that hard-to-say-thing out loud: I love you. But Mom never let me go there. "Oh, wait," she'd say, "*Jeopardy*'s on." And then of course, *Wheel of Fortune*.

When she died, five weeks after her diagnosis, a friend consoled me by saying, "The more you look for your mom, the more you will find her in your heart." This has been true. Ever-present Mom is still there, allowing me to have many a heart-to-heart with her. But here's the deal: Even with almost twenty years of apologizing to her, thinking through our relationship, and realizing what a wonderful mom she was, I know that should we meet up in the great beyond on a cold, crisp day, she will almost certainly suggest I put on a hat and gloves. I will almost certainly be annoyed.

I will, I hope, take a moment to decode her words, and whether I put on the hat and gloves or not, I will respond in kind: "I love you too, Mom."

CONVINCING MYSELF TO BE COURAGEOUS

January 8, 2019

My blog is a kind of parking lot. There I park everything that I'm worried about, and I am worried about a lot as I prepare to travel to Israel with my twelve-year-old granddaughter, Tillie. All the little things that would ordinarily have me nervous when I travel are exacerbated by the fact that my daughter wants me to swallow my fears and project an image of female strength and courage to Tillie. As I prepare to move into Helen Reddy mode—I am woman, hear me roar!—I will try to give away my fear as I write about it here.

But first, let me explain the background of our amazing trip. A year ago, Tillie and I were invited to participate in a year-long, global, intergenerational program for grandparents and their pre-teen grandchildren. It was a pilot program created by the Jewish Agency for Israel. We agreed to meet monthly with our cohorts—three other grandparent-and-grandchild couples. Tillie and I also agreed to spend time together each month to do a fun homework

Chai on Life

assignment. The goal of all this was to build a bond between the two generations. Knowing that kids can't always turn to their parents when they have a problem, I was very eager for Tillie to have a strong connection to me. Hence, I was sold on the concept immediately! That the program culminates in a trip to Israel is a wonderful bonus.

We leave for our trip in four days and here's what I am worrying about (but don't tell Tillie):

1) Foreign currency—I am packing shekels and dollars, but what if I need more cash? On a trip to Europe four years ago, the ATM machine didn't accept my card even though my bank was aware of my travel!

2) Cell phone service—I have spoken to Verizon just like I did the last time I traveled out of the country, but that still didn't make the transition automatic or easy! I have printed out a sheet of instructions this time, but will that work?

3) Electrical adaptors—I ordered Type D ones, just as our tour guide recommended, but they don't look exactly like the picture our leader provided!

4) Going through Customs in Israel—I am a perennial good girl, but on my previous trip to Israel, I got bumped out of line for a more thorough screening (why, oh why?) that felt ominous, separated me from my group, and took forever!

5) Of course, there are a bunch of smaller things that worry me, like hotel hairdryers that are on a different voltage and offer up the possibility of frizzy hair, etc. But those are mundane issues, right? Certainly, I can wear a brave face in handling them??? Right?

I saw a home décor sign at a gift shop recently that is applicable now. It said, "Of course I talk to myself. I need expert advice." In need of a pep talk as I face these issues, I turn to ten motivational messages I posted on social media in the past year:

1) I will not obsess. I will not obsess. I will not obsess.

2) Overthinking: The art of creating problems that don't exist.

3) Feel the fear and do it anyway.

4) Be a warrior, not a worrier.

5) Suck it up, Buttercup.

Chai on Life

6) Tell the negative committee that meets inside your head to sit down and be quiet!
7) Every little thing gonna be alright.
8) Inhale confidence. Exhale doubt.
9) I think I can, I think I can, I think I can.
10) She believed she could, so she did.

Ok, I have parked my worries and filled my tank with confidence boosters. I've also gotten a good laugh, which lightens my mood. (Suck it up, Buttercup?!) Add it all together, and I'm feeling better. It's amazing to see that when I write down my worries, they don't seem as awful as when they roll around continuously inside my brain.

Because of all this, I am going to stop looking at the hole and see the donut instead: An amazing trip with my beloved granddaughter awaits me! The folks at G2family.org have given us meaningful programming so far and will surely provide more in Israel. In fact, I know about one event taking place early in our trip. To prepare for it, the grandparents were given an assignment. We were each asked to write a blessing for our grandchild. The grandkids will receive these handwritten notes in a special ceremony. Here is what I said:

Dear Tillie Rose, I hope you will pick out one wonderful experience from the Israel trip and turn it into a "snapshot" to keep in your mind forever. Then whenever you have a difficult day in your life, you can find that snapshot in your head, and let it shine its light on you. XO, Marmel

This is such good advice, I think I'll follow it too. When I catch myself in an act of personal bravery on this trip, I'll snap a mental picture of it to revisit the next time I am in a panic. Thus, I will be reminded of these facts: I am strong, I am intelligent, I can handle the things that are thrown my way. Indeed, I *am* woman, hear me roar!

NOTE-TO-SELF:

You are brave
and brilliant
and oh so resilient.

Chai on Life

MY STOMACH IS FLAT BUT THE L IS SILENT: A LOVE LETTER TO MY BELLY

August 28, 2022

Dear Belly,

I know in my heart of hearts that I owe you for giving me exactly what I wanted in life: my three kids. I would not trade them for a flat belly. Of course not! Never! Uh-uh!

So, I have compassion — or more likely gratitude. And like loving every gray hair in my head because I earned it, so did I earn this belly.

Thank you.

Thank you.

Thank you.

For Scott. For Shana. And for Lisa.

And then for Avery, Leo, Stella, and Amelia. For Tillie, Lila, and Cici. And for Josh, Dylan, and Jude.

What a large, large gift! Of course, you are large.

Amen. And thank you.

Flawsome:

A person who embraces their "flaws" and knows they are awesome regardless.

SHRUNKEN HEADS VS INFLATED ONES: IN PRAISE OF PRAISE

July 11, 2022

Years ago, when my kids were little, my parents overheard me praising my offspring. A conversation ensued. Mom and Dad claimed such compliments would help swell the kids' heads, while I asked the question: If I don't tell them they're doing a great job, how will they know?

Here's how I knew I was doing a good job as a child: Mom and Dad boasted to Aunt Tillie about my accomplishment. Aunt Tillie then told her daughter, Loie, about it. And finally, Loie told me of the family acclaim. By the way, there are many reasons to love my cousin Loie, but it certainly amplified our relationship for her to be the passer-on of praise to me.

As an adult, I know that I should be able to know when I have done a good job without someone else telling me. But, no, no, no, that's not really how it works for me. I need praise, positive reinforcement, and pats on the back. And if you must give me some constructive criticism, know that my soul will receive it as a put-down, so please serve it with a put-me-up to even the score. Or here's an idea: How about two put-me-ups? That will re-inflate me and get me moving again.

In defense of Mom and Dad's stance, ParentingScience.com shares an article called "Seven Evidence-Based Tips for Using Praise Wisely." In it, they say traditional cultures around the world have always told parents to avoid praise, stating that it could make kids overconfident and too full of themselves.

They go on to claim that things are different today. Today, people think praise can be effective to reinforce good behavior. But it's only good if we use praise *wisely*. For instance, they say to praise kids for things they can control, not for being gifted with special abilities. Such semantics—say it like this, not like this—make my eyes roll. OMG! What happens if we say it unwisely? Oh yeah, we're back to swelling the heads of kids.

I think this is hooey and that we should toss out this nonsense! I stand firmly in praise of praise—for kids and for adults.

Agreeing with me on this topic is Hans Poortvliet of the Netherlands. He is a member of a non-profit called Recognition Professionals International.

This organization is comprised of business professionals who promote the art and science of employee recognition. In the early 2000s, he created a national day for compliments. Its popularity grew quickly and to far-flung countries. It is now celebrated annually on March 1st as World Compliment Day.

An article in the Leiden Psychology Blog touts this holiday and tells us about "The Science Behind Praise." It quotes a study where participants' brains were scanned using an MRI. It found that "receiving compliments led to activation in the reward areas of the brain (the striatum), as similar to receiving monetary gifts."

Had I been hooked up to an MRI, I am sure this next story would have shown my brain to be as lit up as if I'd won the Mega Millions lottery. I was at my folks' house helping them with their computer and printer. Suffice it to say they were terrified of this technology and were clueless about how to solve their problem: a relatively new but infrequently used printer cartridge was not working. This was in the year 2000, so I think it was a phone call to the cartridge company—not a Google search—that instructed me to take the cartridge out, dab it with a wet paper towel, then reinsert it. I followed the instructions, and voila, the printer printed again!

Mom, who had been nervously watching me, shouted to Dad who was in

Chai on Life

another room: "Your daughter is a genius," she said. "Come see what she figured out!"

I had waited a lifetime for this moment! Praise from my parents! In so many words. To my face. Not via the Tillie-to-Loie grapevine. It wasn't shouted from the rooftops, but from the family room. Good enough! And guess what? My head didn't swell. It just got a bit pumped up from its some-times-shrunken state.

Remember the old skit on Saturday Night Live with body builders Hanz and Franz? Their funny tagline was "We want to pump you up!" That's what I want to do too. I want to pump up people through positive comments, recognition, and compliments. And I am not ashamed to say that I want to be pumped up too.

We give journalists Pulitzer Prizes. We give actors Academy Awards. We give scientists and statesmen Nobel Prizes. Likewise, I want to acknowledge the accomplishments of my kids, friends, and self as I stand firmly in praise of praise.

Life 101: A Formula for Living

THE IMPORTANCE OF HAVING A GAME PLAN

January 19, 2018

My financial adviser is a smart guy. He believes that we need to set up rules for my investments and stick to them. The main rule is what percent of my assets is in the stock market and what percent is not. This keeps me from getting greedy (and soon-to-be-slaughtered) when the market is up, and keeps me from getting scared (and running) when it is down.

The main thing about this strategy is that it is a strategy. We don't just behave in a willy-nilly fashion. We have a plan. This concept carries over to other areas of my life, as evidenced by the journal I have kept since January 1, 2005. I make two entries in it each year, both of them on New Year's Day. The first entry details how I spent New Year's Eve so I can look back and remember happy times that would otherwise be forgotten. The second entry records my resolutions for the new year.

Chai on Life

In the early years, I wrote down five or six mundane goals such as "Cut the cussing" and "Take calcium daily," but of course, before long I was forgetting to take the damn calcium. By 2013, one of my resolutions got me closer to a workable plan, closer to a non-willy-nilly strategy. That resolution said, "Do my routine—see card." Then on an index card, I wrote down my daily routine, or at least the routine I followed on my good days.

Here it is in its entirety:

- Go for a walk M-F
- Do 20 minutes of weight training M, W, and F
- Do 10 minutes of yoga T and Th
- Dental care – use electric toothbrush and floss at night, and use regular toothbrush and mouthwash in the morning.
- Nights (M-F) – Use lotion on face, feet, legs, and hands
- Be dressed—with makeup on and hairdo done—within two hours of walking M-F
- Go somewhere daily by noon
- Go to Temple on Friday nights

In the years since 2013, I have had a single resolution—yes, just one. My resolution is to follow my routine. I reinforce this mission by writing, "Make a schedule and stick to it. Without this structure, you are like an unmedicated bipolar patient. For happiness, you need to take this 'drug' daily."

Some may argue that my routine is a whole set of resolutions that is difficult to carry out. But I disagree. I was doing all of these things regularly on the days when life was good to me emotionally, but I failed to do them on down days. So, this gave me a strategy for the up markets and down markets of my life.

I learned the beauty of living this way from my ancestors. My dad—post-retirement—used to have a different activity scheduled daily. If it was Monday, he mentored at an elementary school; if it was Tuesday, he volunteered at Temple, and so forth. My paternal grandmother used to cook a different soup daily. If it was Monday, it was pea soup; if it was Tuesday it was bean soup, and so forth.

When my dad lost my mom, and when my grandmother lost my grandfather, they did not know what to do with themselves! Well, that was the case, but not literally. They at least had a plan for what to do the next day…and the days thereafter. They were not completely adrift. This is the beauty of living life in a non-willy-nilly fashion.

It worked for them.

It works for me.

I recommend it to you!

MOVING A LITTLE BIT AT A TIME TOWARD A RICH LIFE

August 9, 2022

Recently, my morning walk, plus several hours of chasing after five grandkids, plus an evening trip to the grocery store added up to 13,000 steps, according to my fitness tracker! It was shocking to me, but a wonderful reminder of this important life lesson: A little bit + a little bit = a whole lot. This math-fact-of-life is nifty because it applies to every area of life, not just fitness. It applies to finance, friendship, and more. Let me share some examples to illustrate my point and to promote this mindset. It's a pathway to a rich life!

Finance:

A calculator on the Illinois.edu website shows that if a young person saved as little as $20 per week (a bit over $1,000 in a year) and invested it at 10%—which would mean placing it in a mutual fund with a proven track record of at least 10% annual returns over ten years—the investment would be worth $506,326.00 after forty years. That's more than half a million dollars, all attributed to the fact that a little bit + a little bit = a whole lot.

Chai on Life

<u>Friendship:</u>

If you are on the outs with a friend or family member, it's never too late to fix things. A book about divorce will help. The book is *The Good Divorce* by the late Constance Ahrons, PhD. Ahrons identified five kinds of divorced couples and placed them on a continuum: Dissolved Duos, Fiery Foes, Angry Associates, Cooperative Colleagues, and Perfect Pals. She then instructed that if there were one hundred steps from one of these relationships to the next, we should take just one step at a time in the more positive direction. And then of course, another step after that. If we keep going, perhaps Perfect Pal-ship can be ours. All of this is made possible by the fact that a little bit + a little bit = a whole lot.

<u>Writing a book:</u>

If you have ever thought of writing a book but find the task to be daunting, follow the lead of Mike Kahn, a guy in my high school graduating class. Mike is a husband, father of five, trial attorney, and also the author of many novels, among them eleven mysteries featuring detective Rachel Gold. Rumor has it that after work and after the kids went to bed, he wrote one page a night. This means that in a year's time, he could turn out 365 pages. Guess what? The average length of a novel is 300-400 pages. Ta-da! Mike just proved that a little bit + a little bit = a whole lot.

<u>Becoming a successful salesperson:</u>

To build a career in sales, you make a lot of cold calls until eventually you make a sale. Then you make more cold calls boasting of your one sale until you make another sale. Then you make more cold calls boasting of your two sales until you make your third, and on you go. Months and years later, your résumé will show the dozens and dozens of happy customers you have accrued, all because of the fact that a little bit + a little bit = a whole lot.

By the way, don't forget to go back to those happy customers to sell them a second time! And don't forget to ask them for letters of recommendation and referrals. Your next cold call will go a lot more smoothly when you tell them John Jones told you to call. Oh, and by the way, if you tell a potential client that you will call them Tuesday at 2 o'clock, it's a really good idea to call them Tuesday at 2 o'clock. Being a person of your word does a lot to get those referrals and letters of recommendation.

I know firsthand about this method to build a career in sales because I used it successfully to sell myself as a motivational speaker. Over a ten-year period of time, I spoke to over 250 groups in 11 states.

Chai on Life

In summary:

The used-to-be 20-year-old guy who's now a half-millionaire? The person with the renewed friendship? The trial lawyer by day who's a writer by night? The gal with 250 speaking gigs on her résumé? None of these people got lucky. Instead, they got proficient at using this math-fact-of-life.

The really good news is that anyone can use it.

Want to learn to play the piano, guitar, or violin? Practice 15 minutes a day each and every day. Be sure to record yourself stumbling through your piece on day one, so that when you listen to it on day ten, you can be motivated by how much you have improved. Then watch as the mastered sheet music grows into quite a pile over time.

Want to have a collection of china tea pots? Buy one right now and repeat monthly. You'll have twelve teapots in the first year alone because things add up quickly! Soon you will also be collecting shelving units to house your burgeoning teapot collection.

The only hard part in all of this is getting started! So, remember this: If you start today, you will be one step further along than if you start tomorrow.

A rich life can be yours! On your mark, get set, go!

—

PS: The impetus for this story is the shocking fact that this is my 100th blog! I launched my website in September of 2017 with the goal of publishing two blogs or newsletters per month. In these many months, I have written 100 blogs, 19 newsletters, 110 book reviews, and 8 special newsletters for book lovers. I also wrote a total of 47 stories for two other online sources, Worthy.com and Medium.com. It's mind boggling to look back on, but it was easy to achieve. I did it one story at a time. Congratulations to me!

—

When it comes to moving a little bit at a time toward a rich life, my parents always said it this way in Yiddish: A bissel and a bissel machts a groisen shissel.

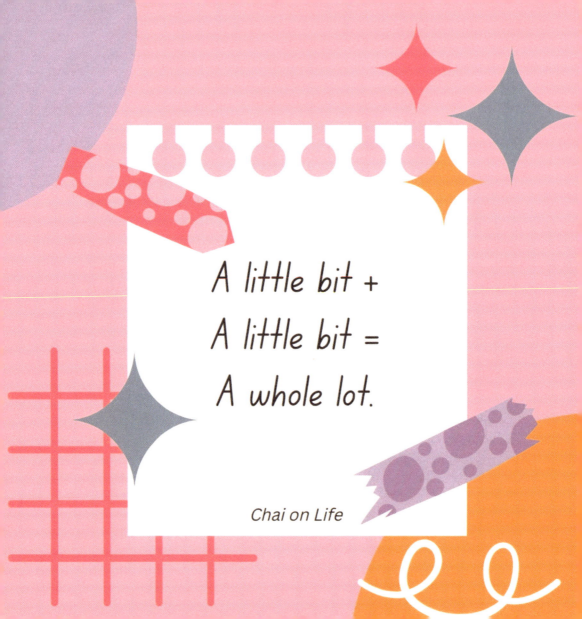

I wrote this story over twenty years ago! All of the details have changed. My kids are grown, married, and have kids of their own. My parents are deceased. I have been divorced for so long that it's no longer an issue. In spite of all the changes in my life—even those brought on by the pandemic—the lesson learned from this story is 100 percent unchanging. It is rock-solid advice that I am proud to share all these years later.

DOING SPLITS AT THANKSGIVING

November 7, 2001

As I begin to think about a personal game plan for this year's Thanksgiving, two memories pop to mind. The first one finds me at Miami University during new student orientation before the start of my middle child's freshman year. As Shana and I sat among hundreds of parents and teenagers, my usually very confident daughter was suddenly overcome with fear about college. Thus, I found her grasping my hand—yes, in public, in front of all those other kids—as she whispered in my ear, "If I could be anywhere on earth right now, I'd be at your kitchen table having a traditional Shabbos dinner."

The second memory finds me at a local elementary school as a substitute teacher for a group of third graders. No matter what I said or did, some upset eight-year-old would raise a hand to tell me that the regular teacher said or did it differently. Before long, I developed a mantra, countering every complaint with the words, "Be flexible!" By the end of the day, three of the little girls actually adjusted to my ways. Gymnasts all, they came up to my desk and dropped into splits as they joyously shouted, "Look, Mrs. Eckert, we're flexible!"

Cute stories, right? But they also teach a lesson—namely, that traditions can bring comfort—that is unless we hold to them rigidly, at which time they can cause pain. Out of the mouths of babes, we also see that joy is to be found in flexibility.

These are great lessons to keep in mind, especially at Thanksgiving when it is so easy to think that our celebration must look exactly like it did in years past in order for us to be content and happy. In reality, life is not a Norman Rockwell painting with the same family members gathered around the same table at the same home eating the same meal.

Things change—especially the people, who pass on, move on, or divorce from the family—and the only constant is that if we allow ourselves to cry over these changes, we will be very sad indeed during the holiday. If, on the other hand, we take all that sameness out and just define a traditional Thanksgiving as "some people getting together for a meal on the fourth Thursday in November," we put happiness within our reach.

Such a definition helps with all elements of the celebration—the who, the what, and the where. Obviously, if we're not attached to the Rockwellian image, we can consider restaurants or the carryout feasts available at grocery stores. And if we're flexible about defining family, we can create a pseudo family from friends when our dear ones are away. Some may ask, "Where exactly are these friends to be found?" And I respond, "It is a fact and not an opinion that the world is full of lonely people waiting for an invitation."

With this mindset, I have found comfort in two very different holiday settings since my divorce. For the twenty years of my marriage, I always cooked a Thanksgiving feast for my immediate family. My parents came in from St. Louis to join us. I still do this in the odd-numbered years that the shared parenting agreement grants me my kids. But in the even-numbered years, when I must be without them, I go to St. Louis instead and invite my

Chai on Life

folks—and all relatives with no other plans—to join me at a local restaurant for a lavish buffet. I find that this version of tradition is equally heartwarming.

As wonderful as this game plan has been and as much as I'd like to stay stuck in it, life sometimes does not permit it. Shana called recently to say that if she could be anywhere on earth for Thanksgiving, she'd be at my kitchen table, but that she is unable to make it home from Chicago. My Scotty called with the same message from New York. Does this sadden me? Well, of course!

But if I waste too much time crying over these empty chairs at my table, I won't be able to find others to fill them. And you know what? I intend to fill them. And I intend to have a wonderful holiday. And when all is said and done, I intend to reward myself with that joyous third grade accolade—"Look, Ms. Eckert is flexible!"

Thus, I do splits at Thanksgiving, remaining limber for the years to come.

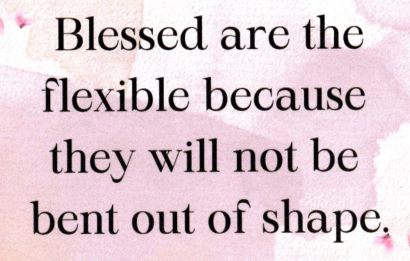

Blessed are the flexible because they will not be bent out of shape.

Chai on Life

GOOD ENOUGH IS GOOD ENOUGH

November 26, 2019

I have a long history of taking something simple and making it hard. Two stories about soup making will prove my point and get us to the epiphany of this tale: If it ain't broke, don't fix it.

I used to make chicken soup frequently. If someone was sick, I'd grab my six-quart pot; add a chicken, carrots, celery, onion, and seasonings; cover it all with water; bring the mixture to a boil; simmer it for two hours, and serve up the broth to the sick person. Oh, wait. I left out a step. I would taste it before I served it to make sure it tasted like chicken soup instead of hot water. If it didn't, chicken bouillon granules came to the rescue, magically altering the taste.

This was my chicken soup strategy for 35 years until my daughter's mother-in-law, Cindy, gave her a cookbook from American's Test Kitchen. Since Cindy is a great cook, and this was a cookbook she was recommending, I gave

Chai on Life

their recipe for chicken broth a try. It was labor-intensive because it involved the repeated handling of four pounds of chicken legs. First, I had to use a meat cleaver to hack those legs into two-inch chunks. Then I had to brown those little pieces in hot oil in a Dutch oven. This was done in batches because they didn't all fit in the pan at once.

Then I added onions, covered the pot, and let it all cook until the chicken "released its juices." Only then did I add water and spices to create the broth. At the end of the soup's cooking time, I had to strain the soup in order to completely pluck those little chicken chunks out. I will confess that the soup was delicious, but I decided never to make it that way again because I am too scrawny to wield a meat cleaver and because browning all of those little chicken chunks was an oil-splattering mess.

Still wanting a new and improved chicken soup, I turned to Ina Garten (The Barefoot Contessa) for her Homemade Chicken Stock. Her recipe starts off with three five-pound chickens that need to simmer with loads of fresh herbs and other ingredients for four hours. Even though boning all that chicken at the end of the cooking time nearly does me in, I have made this recipe many times. But guess what? I still need to taste it before serving it. In spite of all those ingredients, it sometimes comes out tasting like hot water and needs the bouillon granule remedy.

The end result of these culinary misadventures? I vowed not to make chicken soup anymore; it's just too exhausting. All of which makes me wonder: What was wrong with my chicken soup in the first place? After all, it had a 35-year track record of being enjoyed by my family. However, I felt I was cheating to add those chicken bouillon granules, and I am NOT a cheater. The Ina Garten experience teaches me I am not a cheater, I am a resourceful cook instead. It also helps me see these broader life lessons:

- Don't mess with success.
- Leave well enough alone.

Though these are terrific life lessons, I have a problem with them. I have already learned them many times in life, only to forget them and then having to relearn them. Take my hobby of quilt making as an example. I was already a professional quilter, designing all my own unique patterns when I read a book by another professional quilter named Freddy Moran. She famously states that if ten fabrics work well in a quilt, 100 will work better. Because she had a book in print via a major craft publisher, I took her opinion for God's truth and tried a few quilts using her methodology, in spite of the fact that I have difficulty making four or five fabrics play nicely together without clashing. Imagine how difficult it was for me to have 100!

The end result of this sewing misadventure is that I stopped making quilts for about a decade because quilting had become too hard. Fortunately, when my grandkids started to arrive 13 years ago, I managed to pick up the craft again to make baby quilts. Even I knew that a baby quilt had to be simple in nature. Instead of creating an heirloom with hundreds of fabrics in it, I was creating a utilitarian piece ready to face hundreds of cycles in a washing machine.

The question becomes: How am I going to remember these lessons and not screw myself over again in some other area of my life?

And the answer is: I don't know.

However, I am reminded of a favorite book called *Illusions* by Richard Bach. In it, a god figure comes to earth to teach a mere mortal about life. The god tells the mortal that each person is put on earth to figure out the answer to some specific question, stating further, "Here is a test to find whether your mission on earth is finished: If you're alive, it isn't."

So that's where I will leave this—happy to be alive even if it means I will have to go a few more rounds before I finally learn my lesson that better is the enemy of good-enough!

ODD LIFE LESSONS FROM THE GYM

March 12, 2019

Here is a life lesson I learned at the gym: When you go to a birthday party, be sure to eat the cake. I am certain this is not what you were expecting to hear, but then you don't know my personal trainer, Rob Anderson. Yes, he's taught me how to properly do squats, crunches, presses, and the like, but he has taught me much more than that.

Rob owns Custom Physiques in Loveland, Ohio. I go there every Thursday to work out with him for an hour and have done so for over ten years. Beyond the weekly training session, he gives me a twenty-minute routine to do at home three times a week. He also asks me to keep a daily food journal where I record everything I eat and drink. Every week he looks it over and we discuss it.

During one such review years ago, I boasted to Rob that I bravely resisted eating cake at a birthday party. He was disappointed instead of proud. He reminded me that I am NOT on a diet and exercise regimen. Instead, I am living a healthy life in order to have a happy life. Birthday cake is a part of that happy life and therefore it is not to be missed. Just in case you are wondering, funnel cake at the state fair is also mandatory.

Rob's philosophy on eating is the most important thing I have learned in the years we have worked together. When I met him, I was in my mid-fifties. I had always watched my weight and I had a twenty-year habit of walking an hour a day, five days a week to maintain it. During those years, I would repeatedly gain two pounds, then proceed to lose those very same two pounds. However, I had reached a stage where dynamite was required to remove the two pounds that previously came off with relative ease. Simply put, I was afraid to eat. I was enthralled, therefore, when this wonderful man told me I needed to eat six times a day! Let's put four caveats in place, though:

- Your daily allotment of calories does not change in this plan. You just divide those calories up over three meals and three snacks each day. However, once you get your metabolism working again with this system, and once you put on a little muscle mass thanks to exercise, you probably will be able to eat more and not gain weight.

- Rob sees the food world in terms of carbs and proteins. His goal is to cut carbs when possible or to at least balance them with protein. So, if you are dying for a pancake (a carb), that's fine. Just be sure to also order an egg (a protein) with it. And when you are going to a birthday party and planning to eat the cake (a carb), make sure you are protein-heavy the rest of the day.

- Eight cups of water are also mandatory each day. It's ok to drink iced tea, juice, etc., but that doesn't count as water. Also, be sure to show all beverages on your food chart, including coffee and booze.

- And of course, always check with your doctor before you start any new diet or exercise plan.

There is another big lesson inherent in my Rob routine—the importance of accountability. Rob expects me to come to the gym once a week, and so I do. Sometimes, I am not in the mood—and Thursdays sure seem to roll around quickly—but we have this commitment to each other and so I go. Likewise, that food journal keeps me on track. If I eat one of the bank teller's lollipops, I have to write it down. The same is true for the three things I tasted at Costco. And that handful of Goldfish I ate with the grandkids? Yes, I have to report that too. And then Rob and I review it. If I regularly roam too far from "clean" eating, he pulls me back in line. (And my bathroom scale applauds his intervention.)

Chai on Life

But the most joyous lesson I learned at Custom Physiques has to be this: If you join a gym and you go there regularly for weeks and months and years, you are bound to make some friends. Indeed, Rob is no longer just my trainer; he's my very dear friend. I am also great friends with Megan, who trains me when Rob is away. The three of us have been known to eat decadent lunches out together that start with cocktails, move on to tacos or burgers, and end with donuts, ice cream, or once, raw cookie dough a la mode. Yes, we do extra cardio afterwards (I still walk five days a week) and are quick to get back to our normal eating routine in the days following, but for those couple of hours of lunching and laughing, we know what happy living is all about.

Inherent in this tale of over-the-top eating is the fact that Rob trusts me to get back on track with reasonable eating. My favorite story about him further exemplifies this. Knowing that I love ice cream, Rob encourages me to eat it daily. But when my dad was dying—and I was falling apart—Rob told me to eat it twice a day.

Lest you think this Rob guy is perfect, let me tell you this: If I make him aware that I HATE a particular exercise, he is sure to torture me with it frequently! But I'm no dumbbell, so here is a final odd life lesson learned in the gym: Sometimes it's best to keep your mouth shut! Unless of course, you are in the presence of birthday cake...

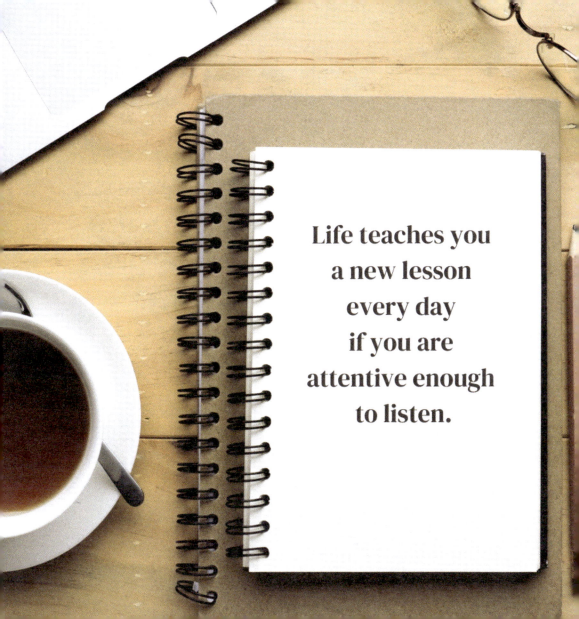

Personal Reinvention

A COVID-19 CORRECTION TO MY VISION

January 2, 2021

I was twelve years old when I attended my paternal grandmother's funeral. The rabbi's words that day set my course for life. Now, at age sixty-eight, I am rethinking that decision and my direction.

The rabbi's words were simple. He said "Momma" was a wonderful wife and mother. My inner voice immediately objected. It said, "That's not enough!"

I'm not sure where such a strident thought came from because I have descended from a long line of stay-at-home moms. My mother, both grand-mothers, and most of my aunts fit this mold, as did my future mother-in-law. Managing a household and raising kids was what women did, and I was happy with that game plan.

It was an unspoken truth that my college degree in elementary education existed as an insurance policy in case my someday-husband someday died prematurely.

Chai on Life

This was all ok with me because all I ever wanted was to be a mom. As a child, I went to a birthday party where we dressed up as our desired future selves. I went as a baby-doll toting Mommy.

Beyond the thought at the funeral, I can recall only one other feminist stirring. I wanted to keep my maiden name at marriage. But when I married in 1973, this was not a common thing to do. I couldn't even imagine a hyphenated last name for my future kids, and without that, I didn't know how the world would connect us. And so, Lorene Elsa Kleiner became Lorie Eckert, and more importantly, by 1983, I became the mother of three kids—Scott, Shana, and Lisa.

I was far too busy raising kids and running a household to think about the "not enough-ness" of motherhood, but my friend Lucy (also a stay-at-home mom) brought it to my attention regularly. She had three kids too—all boys. She often asked me what kind of example I was setting for my daughters to be a stay-at-home mom? (She somehow ignored the lessons our sons were learning.)

When I divorced in 1994, I was ready to take on Lucy's crusade and become something *more*. Because I now had to earn a living on my own, it was nice to have her words fuel my endeavors. And so, as Lorie Kleiner Eckert, I began a career in the motivation field. And I am proud to say that I have been successful. I have four books in print, I have written an award-winning and nationally syndicated column, and I have been a motivational speaker addressing every sort of group from PTAs to Procter & Gamble. I am also a professional quilt artist. I started late, but accomplished a lot in the last quarter century.

It was in August 2020, thanks to a Facebook reminder of what I had posted seven years previously, that I started to rethink this "success." It was a photo of me with my grandson. He was 2 ½ weeks old at the time, and we were lying together on my sofa. He was fast asleep on my chest. The caption read, "Babysitting for Dylan today. Mellow baby, relaxing morning."

While I have always been very involved with my three adult kids and my ten grandkids (currently ages 3-14), babysitting was rarely on my agenda. Because all these loved ones lived in town, I ran Marmel School at my house all day on Mondays for grandkids too young to be in school fulltime. And I cooked family dinners for anyone who wanted to come on Thursday nights. But babysitting per se was not my thing. And while I know I loved that special day with Dylan, I also know I was probably worrying about all the things on

Chai on Life

my to-do list not getting done.

For days after seeing this photo reminder on Facebook, I ached. There were two more grandbabies to come after Dylan. Where are the sweet photos of them asleep on my chest?

And that's when I started to think about Momma's long-ago funeral. That's when I started to wonder if my thinking has been faulty since that day. Is there anything more important in life than taking care of those you love, in Momma's case as a wife and mother?

I recognize that this is in part a COVID correction to my vision. How strange that COVID sufferers may have a diminished sense of taste and smell, while all who live through the pandemic will survive with enhanced vision. I am seeing with new eyes.

You can't go back and change the beginning, but you can start where you are and change the ending.

Chai on Life

REINVENTING YOURSELF:
A HOW-TO

March 26, 2019

Most people do not think of it this way, but we are all experts at reinventing ourselves because we have done it countless times:

- When we graduated from high school
- When we graduated from college
- Or perhaps after getting that advanced degree
- After we got our first job
- After we lost that job
- After we moved to a new city
- When we got married
- Or maybe divorced
- When we became parents

Chai on Life

- And then empty nesters
- After we reached a milestone birthday
- Or maybe we retired
- After the death of a significant other

It's ironic to realize that, in most of these situations, what we thought was a realized goal—the degree, the move, the marriage—was instead ground zero for what comes next. And what does come next? Figuring that out is tough.

The opening song from the musical *Avenue Q* expresses the situation perfectly. In it, a young male character boasts of his new B.A. in English even as he wonders aloud, "What do you do with a B.A. in English?" Even with a positive life change like a newly minted college degree, the way to move forward is still perplexing, even worrisome.

In my latest experience with reinvention, I needed to find myself after the death of my significant other, Big Irv, who died after a four-year battle with lung cancer. It was a stunning loss. I had been worrying about him for so long that I didn't know what else to think about.

I will confess to some months of malaise following his death, though I forced myself to do healthy things like getting dressed daily. Before too long, I remembered there was a second part to recovery—I had to start taking actions to reinvent myself.

I had learned this lesson years ago when I began suffering from empty nest syndrome. The weight of my loss had me pinned to the sofa. At that time, I committed to taking one step a day toward my new life and bought myself a spiral notebook—an accountability log—in which to record my daily actions.

On the first day, I made a phone call to a charitable organization to see what kind of volunteer work was available. The next day, I called another nonprofit. It only took a week or two of similar actions to fill my life with meaningful activity and to blast myself off the couch and away from the tissue box.

As these examples show, the need for reinvention often comes at difficult times in life when we often find ourselves in a muddled state of mind. Thus, my two-step recipe is intentionally simple.

Chai on Life

Step One: Have a daily routine.

Sometimes when faced with change, we just want to pull the covers over our heads and hide, but we can't do that. Therefore, having a daily routine becomes vitally important. Make sure yours includes these healthy things:

Get dressed daily. Ladies, that includes doing your makeup and hair.

Go someplace every day. Being a shut-in is a BIG no-no.

Stay in touch with family and friends—email, text, call, or see someone daily.

Eat nutritious meals and snacks—you have to nourish to flourish.

Practice good sleep habits. Have a set time to go to bed and a set time to wake up. A daily nap is fine, but two might signify depression.

Visit a doctor if you need to. If prescription drugs are called for, there is no crime or sin in accepting such help.

Step Two: Take one step a day toward the new you.

This part might play out differently depending on your reason for reinvention. There are sad/forced reinventions like the ones that take place after you are fired, your boyfriend broke up with you, or you suffered an illness or injury. The happier/chosen reinventions occur when you are in the driver's seat wanting to start a new business, become healthier, find a new relationship, or the like.

If you are going through one of those sadder reinventions, you might have to go hide under the blankets again after you take your initial step, and this is fine, even if it was a teeny tiny step.

For happier reinventions, you might find that taking that first step is invigorating! You might just want to take a second! As you will see, one phone call or Google search will easily lead to another. Perhaps set a timer for fifteen minutes and see how many entries you can make to your accountability log each day!

Clearly, this is a very easy game plan for personal reinvention! The trick now is to get started. Here are some thoughts to spur you towards step number one:

- Accept what is. Let go of what was. Have faith in what will be.
- The first step towards getting somewhere is to decide you're not going to stay where you are (JP Morgan).
- There are seven days in a week, and "someday" isn't one of them.

Chai on Life

- Stop thinking. Stop pondering. Stop strategizing. Stop debating. Go and do!

- The man who moves a mountain begins by carrying away small stones (Confucius).

- You can, you should, and if you're brave enough to start, you will (Stephen King).

- There is no one giant step that does it. It's a lot of little steps.

- You keep putting one foot in front of the other. And then one day you look back and you've climbed a mountain.

- Take that first step. Figure it out from there.

- If you start now, you'll begin seeing results one day earlier than if you start tomorrow.

In closing, please remember this: The new you is just around the bend. All you need to do is keep taking those steps, keep taking those steps, keep taking those steps … towards it. Yes, some will turn out to be side-steps and others will be missteps. It matters not. Just keep stepping.

Eureka!
I Have Found It:
This is Happiness

I'VE GOT IT FIGURED OUT—THIS IS WHAT HAPPINESS IS

March 5, 2021

"What happens when you have everything but it doesn't add up to happiness?" Hoping to start a conversation on happiness with an acquaintance, this was the question I asked. Instead, she was astounded to hear the "having everything" part of my statement, and wanted to know what it's like to feel that way!

Frankly, I was shocked that she was shocked. In my circle of friends, having everything is the norm.

We have:

- Loved ones in our life

- Good health

- A roof over our heads

- Food on the table

- A functional car

- Meaningful work

- Money in the bank

- Leisure time

- Enjoyable hobbies

- All the freedoms America affords

- Plus, freedom from physical, emotional, and sexual abuse

I suspect my acquaintance likewise had all these big-picture elements, and was focusing on the smaller picture instead: THINGS.

Lucky for me, I addressed the issue of THINGS decades ago when I got divorced. Since I was good at home décor and my soon-to-be ex was not, we decided he would keep the family home and most of our stuff, and I would get an allowance to buy a new home and new stuff. This way, the house our kids grew up in would still look like home. I will confess that I ached to leave so many of my possessions behind, but it was clear that having those things had not brought me happiness, so I came to accept that parting with them was not a problem.

Now don't get me wrong. A quarter-century later, that new house of mine is chock full of stuff! And it's been fun accumulating it! But, I have always understood that each acquisition was filling a spot on the shelf, not filling a hole in my heart.

So, what's it like to have everything? It's daunting in an existential way. All excuses are stripped away. I can't say, "If I just had a nicer house, prettier clothes, a flashier car, a great vacation, I would be happy." I have most of that—or I could get it if I wanted it—so why aren't I happy?

But wait, wait, wait! I don't mean to say that I am unhappy, I'm just not *actively happy*.

I realize that's a ridiculous thing to say, and while I am on a ridiculous vein, I'm going to blame it all on my parents. They had all the elements of everything that I listed above, plus they had a full complement of THINGS. Beyond that, I believe they were content, felt no envy, and felt no regret. And yet, when I look back on their lives, I wonder if they were happy? They never labeled it that way.

But speaking of labels, my folks were against using them. Whenever I told one of my kids that they were smart or attractive, my parents bristled.

They feared the kids would get swell-headed! My rebuttal was, "If I don't tell them, how will they know?"

This all reminds me of a novel I read in which the father kept a diary of all the adorable things his daughter said as a child. Once, when she was lucky enough to go with him to run errands, she stood in the middle of the post office, looked around, and asked incredulously, "This is errands?" But really, if he didn't tell her, how would she know?

So, I look around my life of everything and every THING—my life of contentment, my lack of envy, my lack of regret—and I'm thinking, incredibly enough, "This is happiness!"

In my head, I hear the children's song, "If You're Happy and You Know it, Clap Your Hands." It's time to start clapping!

BUT WHAT ABOUT THE FACT THAT LIFE IS DIFFICULT?

March 17, 2021

After writing down a list of all the elements needed to be happy, and after recognizing that I already have all of them in my life, my logical brain figured something out: I'm happy! Quite frankly, I find this astounding…and intimidating. It's shocking because I thought happiness would be something different. Effervescent, for instance. And maybe giddy. And certainly, something that was FELT all day every day. It's frightening because I feel a responsibility to somehow exude happiness. In my mind, this means having FUN. Yet, as a serious student of life, FUN is a concept I know so little about.

But there is a larger problem to explore: How do I factor in my core belief that life is difficult?

This is something I say with regularity because I see and acknowledge pain all around me. In any given room full of people, someone feels

diminished because of their hair, complexion, clothes, weight, etc. And someone else is reeling from a lost job, a failed exam, a bad diagnosis, a breakup, a
death, and on it goes. And truth be told, sometimes I am the person feeling
one of those things!

So, what do I do with this awareness of pain in my own life and in the
lives of others? Ultimately, my dad's life answered this question. In his seven-
ties, he was diagnosed with a bone marrow disorder that required regular
blood transfusions. This led to too much iron in his blood, so he had to have
nightly infusions of an iron chelator. This meant that he spent lots of time in
an infusion center and in the company of home health care workers. Once his
port clogged up, he needed "Human Drano," as the ER nurse called it. He
handled it all using this philosophy: "Everyone has something. This is mine."

So, there it is, my answer: acceptance. Problems and pain exist for everyone, in every life. Period.

In my mind, there is a corollary to Dad's statement: Since problems
are a fact of life, if he hadn't had the bone marrow problem, he'd have had
some other problem. That being the case, we allowed ourselves to get
comfortable with the myelodysplasia since we knew so much about it and
how to handle it.

Extrapolating further, there's also this: In most situations, things could be worse. And then there's also this: Sometimes things get better! In Dad's case, a new drug called Exjade came on the market. An iron chelator in pill form, it freed him from nightly infusions!

So, how do I factor problems into my happy life? I do it with the understanding that pain is part and parcel of life.

This being the case, I can't wait around to find happiness on the other side of pain. I need to find it now.

As I placed those words on the page, two stories about happiness—and chicken—magically popped into mind.

The first stars my daughter as a pre-schooler. Part of our bedtime routine then was for the kids to tell me their "happiest thing of the day." Forty years later, the only response I can still recall came from Shana. One night, without a moment's hesitation, she shouted her answer, "Shicken and corn!" Clearly, she was so young she hadn't mastered the word *chicken*, but happiness? She was bubbling up and flowing over with that.

The second story took place at the end of Dad's life when he lay in a hospital bed waiting to be transported to a hospice facility, where he died a week later. My son, Scott, was with him, enjoying the fact that his grandpa was not only lucid but talkative. When a dinner tray was delivered, Scott fed Dad his supper. The hospital's chicken was so dry and hard to swallow that Dad wondered aloud if the hospital was trying to kill him. Both men laughed. Then they kept the gag running. With each bite of chicken, one of them intoned, "Dry, dry chicken," turning a horrible meal and a wrenching time of life into an unparalleled moment of happiness.

Moments of happiness. Hmmm.

Nothing effervescent.

Nothing giddy.

Nothing felt all day every day.

Something even a serious student of life can find.

But where's the FUN I thought was requisite for a happy life?

I envisioned it as a big bright fiery ball.

Instead, it is glowing embers

Warm enough to heat the Shicken

Even in difficult times.

LIFE ISN'T ABOUT WAITING FOR THE STORM TO PASS, IT'S ABOUT LEARNING TO DANCE IN THE RAIN.

Chai on Life

IS JUMPING NAKED INTO A LAKE THE KEY TO HAPPINESS?

May 22, 2018

My friend Marilynn is known for the funny things she posts on Facebook. A recent one showed an obviously older couple, holding hands, as they jump from a dock into a lake. Adding to the humor is the fact that they are naked and their saggy tushies are in full view. Here are the words that accompany the photo—Marilynn attributes them to Dennis Harshbarger:

I am a Seenager. (Senior teenager.)

I have everything that I wanted as a teenager, only 60 years later.

I don't have to go to school or work.

I get an allowance every month.

I have my own pad.

Chai on Life

I don't have a curfew.

I have a driver's license and my own car.

I have an ID that gets me into bars and the whiskey store.

The people I hang around with are not scared of getting pregnant.

And I don't have acne.

Life is great.

I have more friends I should send this to, but right now I can't remember their names.

On the same day that Marilynn posted this, I put up an image of the Eiffel Tower on Facebook. Alluding to travel, I added the words, "Find out what gives you joy and do it." My headline said, "There are so many reasons to be happy! Please tell me yours." Usually no one responds to my social media prompts, but "MS" responded. Here is our correspondence.

MS: What is the recipe to being happy?

LKE: I always say the recipe is to do less of the things that make you unhappy and more of the things that bring you joy. Lots of things bring me joy—travel, my kids, a good meal, my friends, noticing a sunny day, etc.

MS: Wow, that's amazing. I guess I have to identify the things that make me happy too. But 90 percent of the things in my life make me miserable and kill me inside.

LKE: Think about the 10 percent that don't make you miserable and do more of that. And make sure you do one of those happy things each and every day. In fact, do it first thing in the morning and maybe even write it down in a journal to mark the fact that you did it.

As soon as I sent that suggestion, I berated myself. At various times in my life, I have been in a black hole emotionally, and this Pollyanna-ish answer would have snuffed out any light that I managed to see. So, I wrote a PS.

LKE: Forgive my blithe response. I need to add two things:

If you have health issues, or mental health issues, or if you find yourself in an abusive relationship, or if you have some major problem like that, then I hope you will seek professional help. I have done that, and it has indeed helped.

But for more mundane life issues, perhaps the advice I gave earlier is incorrect. When I told you to DO something that makes you happy, maybe that's asking you to ADD something to an already too busy life. Maybe instead I should suggest that you SUBTRACT something. Are you always pressed for time? Do you have too many things on your to-do list? Do you have too many responsibilities? In short, do you feel like a juggler with too many balls in the air? If so, perhaps the secret to happiness is to allow yourself to put one of those balls down.

At age 66, I find myself stating with regularity that I have never been happier. I have been unable to explain why. But the juxtaposition of these two Facebook posts helps me understand that as a "seenager," I have put down a lot of balls in life.

What gives me joy? Leisure time is high up on the list, right there with no longer having acne.

HOW TO BE RICH IN FRIENDS

February 8, 2021

I have often talked about—and been teased about—the idea of keeping a list called "These People Are My Friends." But I think it's a great idea. When I am flying high emotionally, it helps me figure out the exact right person to join me for a specific adventure. After all, not everyone wants to go on a bus tour, or on a field trip with grandkids, or on a march on Washington. But more important, I have a tendency toward depression. On a day when I am blue, such a list reminds me I am not a social pariah. I am not all alone. I have friends.

Feeling a sense of isolation is a reality during pandemics, so it's important to actively think about and foster friendships. Fortunately, this is something within our control. If we want to be rich in friends, we can be.

As it happens, within a ten-day period in January, three of my dearest friends had birthdays. I continue celebrating them by using them as my examples here.

Chai on Life

Three Great Places to Look for Friends:

1.   Your Childhood—Fan or Rekindle Such Friendships Now

Roberta and I have been friends since kindergarten. Though we have not lived in the same city since 1970, the year we graduated from high school, we talk weekly, and meet each other regularly, often in New York. Roberta is the Dear Abby of my romantic life. She has talked me through high school crushes, 21 years of marriage, and love the second—and third—time around. She also has helped me parse every problem I ever had with my kids or in my professional life, not to mention going through the deaths of our parents together. It's mind boggling but true: She knows more about my life than anyone.

In the last decade, we have further bonded through travel. I feel most comfortable using a tour company and traveling on land, in a bus. She humors my needs and comes along. Hence, Warsaw, Budapest, Vienna, and Prague have been ours, along with fall foliage in all the New England states, and the Grand Canyon, Bryce, and Zion National Parks. Each adventure deepens our relationship and gives us a shorthand for happiness—the merest mention of that hotel with tusks brings a laugh every time.

2. Your B-R-O-A-D Extended Family—You Already Love the Same People, So Love Each Other

Sue is my daughter's mother-in-law. Some people think it strange that we have a friendship, but that's insane to me. We have so much in common! There are five people we both love with all our hearts: my daughter, Sue's son, and our three shared grandsons. In Yiddish, there is a word to describe our important relationship. We are *machetunim*, co-in-laws, and great candidates for friends.

As it turns out, Sue and I are similar in our emotional makeup. We both have up days and down days. As we handled lockdown in Ohio at the start of the pandemic, we called to check in with each other every evening. It astounded me that when she was at the end of her rope, I was managing fine, and vice versa.

With my friend Nancy, I had experienced a similar phenomenon when I was a young mom. We were never homicidal on the same day. It seemed like a blessing then, and again now, to have a dear friend who could help me stay in balance. I will forever be grateful.

3. Any Group You Join Brings the Potential for New Friends, AND You're Never Too Old to Make One

Chai on Life

Vera and I met in a cancer caregivers' support group when we were both AARP gals nearing Social Security. Trust me, I was not looking for friends at that moment. Enraged with my care-receiver for not doing cancer the way I wanted him to, I was a kettle of boiling water, looking to blow off steam. I was at my worst, but Vera liked me anyway, proving that unconditional love is a great element for friendship.

Vera is different from many of my friends because she hails from the world of business instead of one of the helping professions. She's a little tougher. She's a no-nonsense powerhouse with a Git-R-Done attitude. She has lots of ideas for interesting and FUN things to do, and makes all the arrangements for us to do them. Because of her initiative, we participated in two marches on Washington.

As an aside, a man I once dated was an activist. He asked me if I had ever been arrested? This was a crazy question for a perennial good girl like me. "What would I be arrested for?" I asked. "Putting curlers in my hair the wrong way?"

After that, along came Vera, a new friend helping to bring about an adventurous new me—and a couple of bus rides to D.C.

When I look at my "These People Are My Friends" list, I see that it is like a membership list of any organization. Take the Temple Sisterhood, for example. Among its members are very active Board members. There are also women who only come to an event or two each year. And there are those who merely pay dues.

But two truthful things can be said about those women on that list. First, any involvement/support enriches the group. And second, it's possible to take a less active member and turn her into something more.

Thus, I am grateful for my list, and I continue to grow it. It makes me a no-nonsense powerhouse with a Git-R-Done attitude. I know how to fan the flame of friendship. If I want to be rich in friends, I can be.

FLIPPING MY SWITCH

January 9, 2023

When I was a child, I noticed that my mom had two different voices. There was the one she used to talk to my brother, Dad, and me, and there was the one she used when answering the telephone. She was a happy, friendly gal on the phone, but most other times a subdued person. I'm not blaming Mom for being a tired homemaker; I'm learning from her example: Flipping the ON switch in life is always a possibility.

Recently, in the throes of an emotional funk, I decided to flip my switch and to see what would happen. Thus, I signed up for four classes to be held over an eight-week time frame. I learned something from each of the classes, though half the time NOT exactly what the instructor had in mind. There was also the overriding lesson about switch-flipping that I will get to later. But for now, let's enter the classrooms.

Class #1: Creating What's Next

Chai on Life

The title of this five-week class was perfect for me in the aftermath of my recent "retirement." I discovered the class online and signed up for it at 3:00 PM on Wednesday, September 21st. That was exactly one hour after the first class ended. As the perennial good girl, missing a class was odd behavior for me.

Plowing ahead, I put the other four dates on the calendar, only to find I had conflicts for weeks two and three! Forgiving myself, I planned to attend the last two sessions. I made it to the fourth class but had to skip session five when two of the grandkids needed my help.

Clearly, there was no attendance prize for me, but there was a lesson learned: Not everything is stress-worthy. When I sign up to do something fun, there is no reason to make it stressful instead. No need to kick myself. The one class alone was enjoyable. Amen.

Class #2: How You Became You

I loved the title of this class, and I hoped it would explain me to me in a psycho-social sense. Whenever I meet a new friend, I suddenly realize that all my adorable idiosyncrasies are strange quirks to them. I come away from such situations wondering how on earth I got to be this way. I hoped this class would provide the answer.

Imagine my surprise when the topic of the class was human biology! Turns out that we all started as one cell. By the time we were babies, we were composed of 26 billion cells. By the time we were adults, we had 35 trillion cells.

However, I wanted to know why I am so rigid with my daily routine, and how I might un-become those parts of myself that are unbecoming?

I learned a lot from the teacher beyond mitosis: When signing up for a class, I need to read the school's description of the class, not just the title. This one said the presenter was a retired biology teacher who would take us "through the mystery and mysterious functioning of around 200 different cells, beginning with a fertilized egg." A broader lesson reminds me to exercise due diligence in all aspects of life, even when signing up for a one-day class.

Class #3: Aging Well by Eating Well

Hoping to learn that a balanced diet is a cookie in each hand, this class gave me a reality check instead of a chuckle. I actually knew all of this information, but seeing it in one concise list was disconcerting. As we age, we have:

Chai on Life

- Reduced bone mass
- Reduced body water
- Increased body fat
- Reduced muscle mass
- Reduced ability to absorb nutrients

As the instructors—a nutritionist and a med student—discussed these topics, my main takeaway was that exercise, hydration, and a good diet are more important than ever. *Argh!*

But here's a joke to consider: It is said that psychopaths might just be just regular people on a low carb, sugar-free diet.

With this thought in mind, I amend the class's takeaway to include this reminder: Moderation in all things is important, so into every life a little junk food can fall.

Class #4: Speed-Friending

There were twenty people in the class and ten tables. Ten of the participants chose a table at which they stayed for the remainder of the session. The other ten rotated from table to table, visiting each for four minutes of getting-to-know-you conversation. Then a bell rang, and it was time to move on to the next table and the next new friend-to-be.

This turned out to be loads of fun and slightly crazy. Each time we moved to a new table, the din in the room got louder as we got more accustomed to what…being friendly? Actually, we were like my mom at the start of the story; we put on our telephone voices and adjusted our dials to a happier frequency.

And that's the main takeaway from this four-class adventure…

Flipping the ON switch in life is always a possibility. Even signing up for classes was flipping a switch. Remembering to put on the friendliest version of myself was flipping another. I'm not going to say my emotional funk is now gone, but I will say this: It wasn't present during my ON-ness.

More classes may be in my future. Stay tuned…

Some Odds
and Ends
to Mention

DECIPHERING HILLEL THROUGH THE YEARS

February 19, 2021

A guiding principle of my life has been the famous quote from Hillel that sets out a three-part harmony for living: If I am not for myself, who will be for me? If I am for myself alone, what am I? And if not now, when?

Understanding the last part of the quote has caused me great difficulty. From teen years to today, I have interpreted it four different ways.

When I was young, I took it as a restating of what my parents always told me: Don't put off until tomorrow what you can do today.

But then I hit the age of 40 and watched as my beloved Bubbie declined in health. I imagined her as an hourglass and tried to find a way to keep the hourglass on its side. I wanted to retain those last precious grains of sand. But of course, that wasn't possible. Time ran out. In losing her, this part of Hillel's saying took on a new meaning: No one is guaranteed tomorrow, so we have

Chai on Life

no choice but to make the most of today.

A couple years later, this meaning morphed again as I re-entered the workforce after a 21-year hiatus as a stay-at-home mom. Painfully aware that everyone had a two-decade head start in résumé building when I entered the race, Hillel's words gave me a sense of time urgency and an impetus to accomplish things in life.

It is in this stage that I am stuck.

In my current interpretation, Hillel has stopped being a bearded and kindly elder and become a stern taskmaster instead. As my inner drill sergeant, he needs me to accomplish things! Now!

Theoretically, this tough guy believes that if I scratch a few things off my to-do list, then I can pursue pleasurable activity. In reality, there is always so much on the to-do list that leisure time never comes, or when it does, it feels like stolen moments wrapped in guilt.

As I deal with my sense of time urgency, I think of a job I once held. Most of my working years found me self-employed, doing motivational work. But there was a year when I felt the need to supplement my income and got a job as an administrative assistant to the president of a real estate investment trust.

This company owned apartment buildings. One of my tasks was to write a policy manual for our apartment managers. No matter what section I was writing—how to vet prospective tenants, how to replace air conditioners on the fritz, how to hire subcontractors—my boss told me to instruct the managers to do that task with a sense of time urgency! I scoffed at this, knowing that not every job merited that approach.

But even as I belittled his thought process, I knew this was my approach to my private life and it has remained that way for years.

It's been exhausting.

A change is called for.

And yet…

My biological clock is ticking, and I am not guaranteed tomorrow. I shouldn't put off until tomorrow what I can do today. But as I think of racking up more accomplishments, I understand that professional doings will not appear in bullet points on my grave.

Those things don't get written in stone.

Here's what does:

Mom. Marmel. Friend.

Chai on Life

And so, I rethink Hillel once again. Perhaps it's a two-part, not a three-part, harmony. Perhaps a stand-alone third part dictating now-ness is a figment of my Type A imagination. Instead, perhaps I am to take care of others now, while also taking care of myself … now.

I know what it means to take care of others. With 40-plus years of mom-hood, that's not a problem. I'm experienced at that.

But, what about the instruction to take care of myself? Pleasurable activity without guilt comes to mind, though I am not at all experienced at that.

Perhaps it's time to make this a goal and master it.

I'm sixty-nine years old; if not now, when?

SELFCARE:

The radical notion that you deserve your own attention.

Chai on Life

IN A BILLY JOEL
STATE OF MIND:

A Story about Anger and Forgiveness
October 25, 2021

I went to a Billy Joel concert the other night. His wonderfulness is a story for another day. Today, I want to talk about his song "Big Shot," and use it as a springboard for discussing forgiveness. To fully cover this topic, I'm going to draw Carly Simon and Frank Sinatra into the mix.

"Big Shot" is one of Billy Joel's greatest hits, and its lyrics are full of anger. According to <u>Vulture</u> (a section within *New York Magazine*), it is "the most pissed-off record Billy Joel ever made." The narrator is enraged with his friend for things that happened the evening before. The friend had to have the last word! And the spotlight! And seriously crossed a line when opening up his (her?) mouth! The narrator repeatedly shouts, "You had to be a big shot, didn't you?" Those last two words famously get slurred and become "dintcha."

When Billy Joel performed this song at the concert, I was interested to hear the intensity with which the audience—yes, me included—joined in on the sing-along. We knew every single word. This made me wonder: Does everyone have a Big Shot in their life to shout about?

Going from dintcha to dontcha, I started to think about Carly Simon's song "You're So Vain." Apparently, she is addressing an ex-lover when she says, "You're so vain, I bet you think this song is about you." And then she asks twice in a row, "Don't you? Don't you?"

Biography.com says, "Ever since Carly Simon released her accusatory track in 1972, the identity of the 'you' has remained one of the greatest mysteries in music history." I recognize that this is a great gimmick for promoting the Carly Simon brand, but on the other hand, since the song came out in 1972, that's almost 50 years of carrying that particular grudge. What a heavy load to carry for half a century!

Speaking of old grudges, there is the one surrounding Frank Sinatra's song, "The Best is Yet to Come." I learned of it when I wrote a story about the crooner.

When Sinatra died in 1998, he had been married for almost twenty-two years to his wife Barbara. She was the one who created his tombstone. It included the inscription, "The Best Is Yet to Come." It also called him a "beloved husband and father." This marker remained in place until 2020, when someone took a hammer to it to remove the word, "husband." Damaged beyond repair, there is a new marker now. It says, "Sleep Warm, Poppa."

Clearly, there is still a feud between Barbara and the kids. This is ridiculous! Here's why: He died over 20 years ago. Barbara died too, in 2017. But the more important chronology is that Sinatra's surviving kids were born in the 1940s. Shouldn't they be mature adults by now? And since all the key players in their family feud are dead, the Sinatra kids effectively prove the old adage that grudges seldom hurt anyone except the one bearing them.

I am thinking about the giving—and receiving—of forgiveness because the Billy Joel concert was September 10, 2021. It was smack dab in the middle of the Jewish high holiday season that includes Rosh Hashana and Yom Kippur. Rosh Hashana is the Jewish New Year. Yom Kippur is the Day of Atonement. During this ten-day period, we actively make amends with those we harmed in the past year and ask God for forgiveness.

In a Yom Kippur service long ago, the rabbi gave all the kids in the congregation a Magic Slate. Remember that toy? It was a two-layer tablet with a thin plastic sheet on top. You could write or draw on it, but when you peeled back the plastic sheet, everything you had drawn was erased. The rabbi had the kids draw a picture of some behavior they regretted from the past year.

Chai on Life

Then he had them lift the thin film, thereby giving them a blank slate for the new year. Better still, he told them in so many words that they were forgiven.

But here is the takeaway from the story: God is not just granting forgiveness to the kids, but to everyone. This would include the big shot, the vain guy, and the person who had the audacity to love my loved one. And if God can forgive them, I must too. Otherwise, I am holding people to a higher standard than God does. Talk about ridiculous…

Oh! And here's some good news: This same thought process applies to things I have done for which I have trouble forgiving myself.

I get it that Billy Joel—and Carly Simon—will continue to sing their hit songs. Of course, they will! But for the rest of us not earning royalties on our anger, it's time to realize what a heavy load we carry when we carry a grudge.

It's time to wipe the slate clean.

IS THERE A STIGMA TO GETTING PSYCHOLOGICAL HELP? I DON'T FEEL IT!

January 10, 2018

I started to see a psychologist when my oldest child was 14. I saw that psychologist, Pam, for 21 years. I would have seen her longer except that she retired six years ago. I feel absolutely no stigma in reporting this. I am not ashamed that I sought such help. In fact, I may be boasting. I am very fortunate that for all those years, I had a paid professional friend to help me through the ups and downs of life.

Pam was great. Yes, she helped me climb out of a couple of emotional black holes I managed to fall into through the years. But, for the most part, there were no black holes. She just helped me deal with ordinary stresses, even though mine has been a privileged life.

My presenting problem was not that my child was into drugs or alcohol. Nor was he flunking out of school or hanging out with a gang. My problem

Chai on Life

was that he often needed a ride home from the mall just as I, a stay-at-home mom, needed to cook dinner. Of course, it always meant going out into rush hour traffic. It drove me nuts, which of course is ridiculous in retrospect.

Before I go on, let me beg forgiveness of those moms who would have larger things to worry about:

- like not having a reliable car
- like not having money to buy gas
- like not having food to put on the table
- like getting home from work in rush hour traffic in order to cook

Apologies in place, I will defend myself for being stressed in spite of being very fortunate. Toward this end, I share a report I once heard on NPR about having enough money in America. The reporter started out interviewing a family in a middle-class income level and moved up and up through various income levels until he reached a family earning a million dollars a year. Guess what? At every level the family was stressed out as it struggled to pay for all they felt was essential in life. Granted, at the lower income level money for room and board was a stressor while at the million-dollar mark boarding the horses was at stake. Nevertheless, all felt stress.

One of the things I have learned about life is that having *every thing* is NOT equal to having *everything*, and that being privileged does not make you immune from unhappiness. The recent suicides of Kate Spade and Anthony Bourdain teach us this. It's a fact: In every life, there are hiccups in happiness. What to do? I advocate seeking professional help as needed.

In my own case, there were times I saw Pam weekly, and times when I saw her monthly, and times I just checked in with her every couple of months. There were also times when I thought I was done with counseling, but she disagreed. And there were times when she thought I was done with counseling, but I disagreed. And then 21 years later, she retired, and I am handling things just fine on my own. Of course, after all the years of this unique friendship, her voice echoes in my head and guides me still.

Recently, I saw a cute Bag Tag by Suzy Toronto. It says, "New shoes… cheaper than therapy and a whole lot more fun!" I chuckled and let out a sigh of relief that I am in a stage of life when new shoes can cure the blues. But rest assured that if this form of therapy should stop working, I will phone my internist to get a referral for the real deal!

Suicide and Crisis Toll-Free Lifeline: 988

THAT TIME I NEEDED
A HUSBAND

September 21, 2020

In June, the HVAC guy came to do an annual checkup of my air conditioning system. Lots of hours after he left, I went to get something in the basement—I have a one-story house with a walkout finished basement—and found a water spot in the middle of the family room carpeting. It was about three feet in diameter. Forgive me, but my first thought was that the guy had had a potty accident.

My second thought was to realize that he used the outside faucet to clean the A/C filter. If the pipe behind that faucet had frozen and broken during the winter, water could flood into the basement when he turned it on. But in the middle of the family room? That made no sense!

Before anyone gives me credit for my plumbing knowledge, let me explain: That pipe had frozen and broken twenty years ago, and watered one of the bedrooms in the basement. Experience being a wonderful thing, I went

Chai on Life

to look in that bedroom. There was another water spot there, and about the same size! I quickly made sure the faucet was turned off. It was! Whew! And luckily me, there were only two water spots. But one in the middle of the family room? That made no sense!

After grabbing four beach towels from their storage place in the garage, I went to sop up the water. Approaching the carpet on hands and knees, I realized that the carpeting, which looked dry, was not. Instead of having two independent water spots, I had one huge spot. It encompassed a fourth of the bedroom floor and a third of the family room floor, not to mention the fact that there was a hole in the wall that connected the two rooms, perhaps from gushing water.

My first reaction was to laugh because my fear had been there might be a mouse in that stack of towels from the garage and that THAT would be my problem. My second reaction was to yearn for a husband, any husband, to handle the crisis.

To all of my feminist friends, and to my daughters and granddaughters, I know that women are capable of handling issues like this. And I did go on to handle it. And I am proud of that fact. But what my inner voice was screaming through the early part of the adventure was this: I DON'T WANT

TO DO THIS MYSELF!

Hissy fit aside, I called my insurance company, and got the ball rolling on my claim. By 10 PM, I had a water extraction company in the basement sucking up water.

The next day, they were back, tearing out wet carpeting and padding, removing wet baseboards, and setting up huge fans to dry things out. One of the demolition guys asked me which baseboards to remove. I was speechless. Not only do I have no knowledge of carpentry, but as I stood there, woozy from the ongoing destruction, I felt like a patient in the ER coming back to consciousness. How could the doctor be conferring with me about what he should do next?

Of course, this thought was a gift from God. It was a reminder: "Lorie! It's your basement, not your body, that's wrecked! Be grateful!"

Through those first couple of days, I calmed myself with the thought that everything would be back to normal within two weeks. Such a strange thought! Certainly, a throwback to that old movie *The Money Pit*, where the humorous refrain to every question about when a given project would be done was always, "Two weeks!" But I'll tell you what: Within two weeks, I was no longer in shock.

Chai on Life

How did I accomplish that? Time passed. How did it pass? To forget my woes, I got lost in jigsaw puzzles. When puzzles didn't work, I went to sleep. (PMS taught me long ago that sometimes sleep is the only answer.) I made no demands on myself to do any work other than respond to the insurance adjuster and then to the restoration company. With each meeting/call, I made the decision at hand. One step at a time and one day at a time, I was restored to normalcy, and the basement was scheduled for a similar fate.

When I finally got back to work, to my blogging, I was amazed to see that the story I had been writing before the calamity was about my mom's stellar handling of frozen pipes when I was a child! This coincidence helped another pop to mind: Mom and Dad once dealt with extensive water damage. The condo above theirs had a major fire, and the water that saved the neighbor's condo nearly destroyed theirs.

As I chatted with my brother about this, he reminded me that the result of Mom and Dad's catastrophe was a gorgeous home, completely remodeled and redecorated. He encouraged me to adjust my frame of mind, to think of my mishap as a good excuse to redecorate, and to enjoy the process. He's my big brother, so I listened.

I am grateful for the mindset he provided and for the insurance policy that helped me act on it. I am also grateful for all the other family members and friends who kept calling to encourage me—to make sure that I did not feel all alone—as I handled the situation.

Eleven weeks have passed since the pipe burst. If you ask me when my beautiful new basement will be complete, I'd have to say "two weeks." I chuckle at the thought…and appreciate my return to laughter.

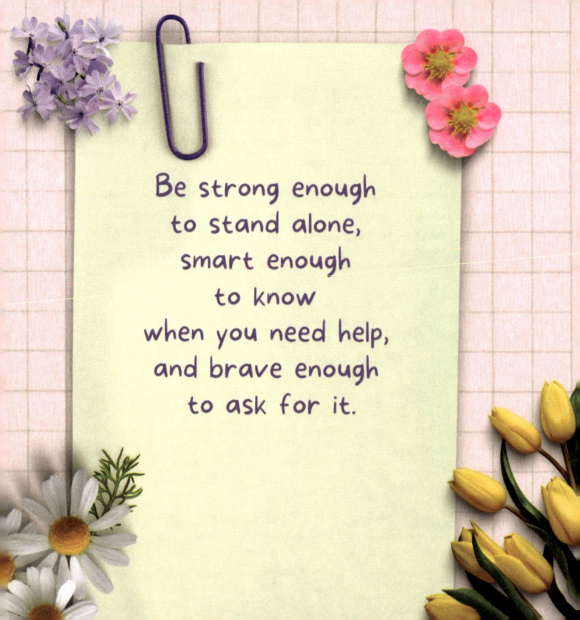

THREE REASONS TO
WRITE IN A JOURNAL

August 27, 2019

Here are three beliefs I have:

Whenever I talk about one of my problems, I give a piece of it away.

I have an inner voice to guide me in life.

If I want to remember something, I better write it down.

Combining these three beliefs, it is only natural that I am keen on using a journal to navigate life. Let me tell you how journaling has helped me...as I suggest it to you.

Journaling as a means of talking out a problem:

When I tell a friend my problem, I give a piece of it away. The same thing happens when I tell myself the problem by writing it down in a journal. I once had a "friend" state that the problem with me is that I have to talk about every problem twice. This is not true! I actually have to do it three, four, or five times! While I would never dare to burden friends with the same problem repeatedly (I hope), I can go on and on about it in a journal ad nauseum.

Wow! Like the *plop, plop, fizz, fizz* of Alka-Seltzer, what a relief that is!

For me, there are two ways to write in a journal. One is to pretend I am talking to a friend. Thus, I write down the words as if I were speaking them. There are times, however, that I don't really know what's wrong. I just feel so darn agitated! In these situations, I do a writing sprint. I give myself a writing prompt such as "I feel miserable because_____." Then I set a timer for five or ten minutes and start to write. My rule is this: I must keep my pencil moving on the page continuously until the timer rings to end the session. While most of what I write comes close to being gibberish, there will always be at least one little bit of wisdom that I will highlight in yellow. During my next journaling session, I can pop open that little kernel of truth.

Journaling as a way to make major life decisions:

If you have ever made a list of the pros and cons of taking an action, you will understand this use of a journal. The beauty of writing the list here is that it will not only be preserved for future reference, but you will know where to find it! The importance of saving the list is this: If the decision proved to be a bad one, you have the whole list of determinants at hand to examine—and steer clear of—in the future. If on the other hand it was a good decision, your blueprint for success has been immortalized.

In my younger days, I used to meditate to get in touch with my true thoughts before making such a list. As I have gotten older, that still small voice inside of me has gotten louder and guidance is readily available. I just have to access it. How to do that? Easy! You just Get Quiet and Listen. Both systems will work. I encourage you to give them a try.

A final thought about major life decisions: In making your lists, it is fair to include the opinions of your friends and family members. But remember: When we are talking about YOUR life, we need to compare it to a ride in a car, and you need to be the driver, not the passenger. Clearly, your vote carries more weight than anyone else's. Got it?

Journaling as a way to remember the highlights of my life:

Recently, I was talking to my eight-year-old grandson about his other grandmother who helped him create an enormous stuffed toy. I said to him. "You're really lucky. You've got a very special grandma." He responded, "Two very special grandmas, actually." As much as I would like to think that I would remember these words ALWAYS, the truth of the matter is I have ten grandchildren, all of whom say adorable things, and it's hard to remember it all.

Chai on Life

That's why I write it down in a journal. This type of journaling is an emotional picker-upper for me. It's the place I come to when it's a rainy day inside my head and I need to find sunshine.

I also keep a journal of the highlights of my professional life. My current goal is to become rich and famous due to the success of my new book, *Love, Loss, and Moving On* (!!). But like the talented high school athlete aspiring to play pro football, that's probably not going to happen. It's important therefore to remember all the little successes I've had, to view them as the tiny miracles they are, and to be grateful. It is said that most overnight successes took ten years to achieve. The journal helps me stay in the game, just in case a major league recruiter is around the next corner.

So, there you have it—the three different ways I use a journal. Sometimes, I employ all three uses, such as when my dad was dying. Though my friends tried to help, their words got nowhere near my pain. I was so all alone in my misery that I didn't know where to turn. So, I started a journal called, "What my friend would tell me…if I had a friend" and then I said all the words I needed to hear.

Yes, I talked through many problems in that journal. I also weighed the pros and cons of many huge decisions including hospice care. But there is other stuff parked there that I can only appreciate now, years after the horrible experience: My friends and other loved ones really were there for me. They said beautiful things in emails and text messages that I printed out and saved in that journal, that receptacle, that permanent record of my life's journey.

You, too, can have such a treasure. It's just a journal away.

Aging

BEING THE PATIENT VERSUS THE VISITOR IN THE EMERGENCY ROOM

June 11, 2019

"If your heart stops, do you want us to resuscitate you?" Being asked this question at 2:30 AM was one of the most disconcerting things that happened to me two weeks ago. Nurses were just getting me settled into my newly acquired hospital room.

Even four-and-a-half hours in the emergency room with symptoms suggestive of a stroke or heart attack did not rattle me as much as that question. Here I was, thinking my symptoms were a fluke that would resolve themselves by morning, when this question took me someplace else instead. My answer was swift and emphatic: "Yes! I'm *only* sixty-seven years old! Resuscitate me!"

Emergency room vigils are all too familiar to me, having presided over my dad's health before his death in 2010. He once had six ER visits in four weeks! One of the oddest things about last weekend's experience was to realize that I was the care *receiver* instead of the caregiver. All three of my children

Chai on Life

plus my son's significant other watched over me in the ER, making perfectly clear to us what I missed back there in 2010: I am no longer a member of the sandwich generation. I am now a slice of bread. When a hospital admission finally took place, *they* were the ones who got to go home, wondering and worrying about what tomorrow would bring, hoping, of course, that I wouldn't be toast. (Sorry, I couldn't resist. I must be feeling better, right?)

As my hospital journey continued through Saturday with a whole day of tests and waiting for test results, my daughters kept me company, chatting away at the foot of my bed and setting off memories of the good old days when I was the visitor instead of the visit-ee. Thus, I recalled the late September day I spent with Dad at the skilled nursing facility where he lived. Since it was a sunny, warm day I took him outdoors in a wheelchair. In his inimitable style, he fell asleep immediately. Before long, two women entered our court-yard area pushing an elderly woman on a rolling bed. They parked the bed and positioned themselves on either side of her. As they conducted a conver-sation across her soon-to-be-sleeping body, I had no choice but to listen in.

I learned that I was in the presence of a mother and her two daughters. One of the sisters lived nearby and the other was visiting from far away. Love flowed as they had a delightful time catching up with each other and sharing family news. I was moved to think that one day my daughters and I would be the characters in a similar play. I just didn't imagine it happening so soon, at age sixty-seven.

I can say with all honesty that it was nice to see my daughters at the foot of my bed making jokes with each other and with me, but if I have a vote in the matter, next time I want to enjoy togetherness at one of the grandkids' dance recitals, band concerts, or choral concerts. (Are you listening, God?)

Ultimately, I was discharged. After a conversation about whose house I would go to, I made sure my house won. My daughters drove me there, fed me dinner, and tucked me in for the night. Then, with great trepidation, they left. I knew how they felt because this was an exact replay of the time I brought Dad home from the hospital to his place in an independent living facility. As I pulled his apartment door closed, I stood in the hallway and wondered how he could possibly be safe on his own, but then again, I didn't have a Plan B.

Beyond knowing what my daughters were thinking, I now had Dad's mindset as well. He was terrified of all the what-ifs running through his head. I hope he knew to sleep with the lights on because ghosts and goblins only appear in the dark.

Chai on Life

When Dad was in independent living, my kids and I thought it was ever so cute that every morning he had to hang a smiley face sign out on his door handle to let the staff know he was alive and well. Such a desire to know is now ours. Thus, I am the proud owner of the newest Apple Watch that has an SOS system built in. It is automatically set to call 911 in an emergency, plus it will notify each of my kids via text.

Nine days in to this medical odyssey, we still have no diagnosis, though many dreadful things have been ruled out. I am able to resume my normal life, albeit with a dash of apprehension. It is my hope that ultimately the purchase of the Apple Watch will prove to have been (you'll love my word choice) overkill. But I have the watch now. And it's lovely! It's so stylish! And so befitting a sixty-seven-year-old woman who still has a lot of living to do!

Choose life and live it.

Chai on Life

STILL YOUNG ENOUGH TO HAVE A CRUSH

December 26, 2017

There's this man. I guess I'd have to say I have a crush on him. He's my age and he's tall with a wiry build. He still has hair—it's wiry too. And a mustache. I like mustaches. I see this guy every two years. When I say that I see him, I mean he's on a stage and I'm in the audience. He is a cantor, a Jewish clergyman/musician, and he always performs at the biennial conference of the Union for Reform Judaism (URJ). I attend this event to have the extraordinary experience of worshipping with five thousand fellow Jews.

Beyond having a crush on this music man, I feel for him. There's a whole cadre of Jewish musicians these days who are making magic with the liturgy. He was in the forefront of this movement, because he wrote new melodies for old prayers. How does he feel on a stage full of fellow practitioners as he becomes the elder statesman and as they further blaze his trail? It was the young musicians who led our night of music. They paid tribute to him, let-

Chai on Life

ting him sing one of his "greatest hits," but how does that feel?

There was another musician on the stage that I felt for too—he's about twenty years younger than my heart throb. I've also watched this guy over the years. He was so young at the start! And it was amazing then—and now—to see the teenage component of the URJ literally jump up and down as they sang every word along with him. Years ago, he jumped up and down too—through the whole song! This year, I noticed that he started the jumping, but soon let the kids continue without him. And of course, there is now an even younger guy on stage who is following in his footsteps. How does that feel?

As much as I'd like to convince myself that I'm writing about professional jealousies here, what I'm really talking about is aging. But that's such a heavy topic to draw from this evening of musical joy. We sang along! We danced in the aisles! We clapped with our hands high overhead! And we loved every moment! There were religious songs and patriotic songs and since we were in Boston, we even sang the "Cheers" theme—so happy were we to be in "a place where everybody knows…our tribe."

At one point, I found myself sobbing with joy in the arms of my dear friend, Liz. She's an emotional gal, too, so we bubbled over together as delirious as if were drinking champagne. And as she held me, I saw a beautiful sight over her shoulder. The man behind us, a decade or so older than us, the one she had just told me about, the one in a late stage of cancer—he was grooving to the music, pretending his cane was a guitar, and strumming away for all he was worth.

Our song leader brought us down from a musical high and tethered us together by closing the show with a song that invites arms around each other and gentle swaying. Thus, we sang a prayer used to mark joyous occasions. It thanks God for giving us life, for sustaining us, and for enabling us to reach the happy season. And so, the older musician, and the younger one, and the younger one still, and the teenagers, and the grown-ups, and my group of baby boomers, and those older still— regardless of our age, we all found ourselves thanking God for being alive.

MY PERSONAL STATE OF THE UNION ADDRESS

May 12, 2020

Here's a little history lesson, and then I'll get personal. In January or February or March of each year, the President of the United States gives a State of the Union Address to a joint session of Congress. Did you know this address is *mandated* by the Constitution, and it is considered a *duty* of the President to do this? In this message, the President is supposed to talk about important issues facing America as well as offer ideas for solving the nation's problems. This directive from our founding fathers intrigues me. Clearly, it speaks to the importance of taking inventory in life. Since the concept seems equally useful for individuals, I offer my own Personal State of the Union address (PSOTU) now.

As a 68-year-old woman, here are the issues facing me:

1) I am suffering from little-piece-of-paper syndrome.

2) My body seems to be holding up okay, but my 34-year-old-house? Not so much.

Chai on Life

3) I can't keep up with everything I need to keep up with.

4) Death has started to visit my friends.

5) In the face of these struggles, gratitude comes to mind. Thank God for my loved ones who help put life in perspective.

Issue #1: I am suffering from little-piece-of paper syndrome.

I have always written notes to myself for things I need to remember. I don't claim to have dementia, just coping with the natural aging process, but the older I get, the more little notes I need to write. These little scraps of paper cover the kitchen counter and my bedroom dresser, plus I tape them to my bathroom mirror, computer screen, and my car's dashboard. If it's really important, I hang it on a 12-inch piece of tape in the kitchen doorway to hit me in the face when I enter. I even have a file folder called "Little Pieces of Paper." It's ridiculous and it's overwhelming. Are my cognitive skills slipping?

Issue #2: My body seems to be holding up okay, but my 34-year-old-house? Not so much.

I have needed major home repairs every year for the last four years. This year, I'm replacing the wood siding on two of four exterior walls. The expense is shocking, but equally difficult is finding competent people not only to bid the work but to actually come out to do it after I sign on the dotted line. As I complain about this to my son, his response is the same every time: I should sell this place and move elsewhere. Is he implying a newer house or a residence for older people?

Issue #3: I can't keep up with everything.

Beyond email, which is a 24/7/365 problem, there is the issue of snail mail. I have long ago stopped getting paper statements from companies that get paid automatically via credit card or bank debit, but statements from credit card companies, banks, financial institutions, health, life, and home insurance companies litter my life. Add to that letters of solicitation from charities I support, magazines from AARP and AAA, renewal notices for my auto license, my theater subscription, my safe deposit box, and the like, and I am swamped. Remind me of an upcoming wedding to buy a gift for, or those miserable but annual tax returns to file, and I am flipping out. Are we living in an increasingly complex world, or am I falling behind because I am an exhausted old lady?

Issue #4: Death has started to visit my friends.

Chai on Life

I have gone through lots of stages in my thoughts about death. I spent some time as a child being terrified of death. Then I had kids and made a deal with God: I would be okay with dying if He/She would just let my kids stay alive and be well. Then I watched my mom die in cancer-caused pain and watched my dad die of old age. In both cases, I learned there are things worse than death. I will miss the healthy, vibrant version of them every day of my life, but that version was no longer an option.

My sister-in-law just died at the age of 72. She had reached the stage of "no options" and explained that fact to her kids. She instructed them to have a funeral for her, throw dirt on her casket, have a celebration of her life, and then go on and live their own lives. Her courage and strength in the face of death help me get more comfortable with the thought of death.

Issue #5: Thank God my loved ones help put life in perspective.

2019 was a big year for our family. My oldest grandchild, Tillie, became a Bat Mitzvah, and my son and his lovely girlfriend got engaged. This kind of news went right into the annual Christmas letter. But equally important—or maybe more important—are all the lesser occasions when we shared togetherness. Before the coronavirus, it was the grandkids' band concerts, soccer games, and the like. It was family dinners and holidays together.

During coronavirus times, it's Zoom meetings, FaceTime chats, drive-by parades for birthday celebrations, and standing together outside—and six feet apart—to converse. It's being emotionally close in spite of being physically apart.

All ten grandkids have taught me things this year, but let me mention the youngest and the oldest:

- Baby Jude is newly three years old. He and his parents love the Beatles. Currently, he pretends to be John Lennon (and allows me to be Paul De-Cart-Me) as he sings "All You Need Is Love" on a continuous loop during our Zoom time together. His voice is as sweet as the song's lesson.

- My Tillie is newly 14 years old, and in the last few months, she has surpassed me in height. Before the coronavirus, as I stretched to place a kiss on the top of her head, I ached. She is a graphic reminder that the kids are growing up, that time is marching on.

As I review the five issues in my PSOTU, I notice a pattern. Each one ends with some awareness of aging. For months now, I've had one foot in the grave! The coronavirus, with its very real threat to my age group, is a much-needed reminder to be fully alive while I still have the chance. Little pieces of paper and home repairs be damned!

With this new understanding, I resolve to pluck that one foot out of the grave and keep it moving forward, promising a full report in next year's PSOTU!

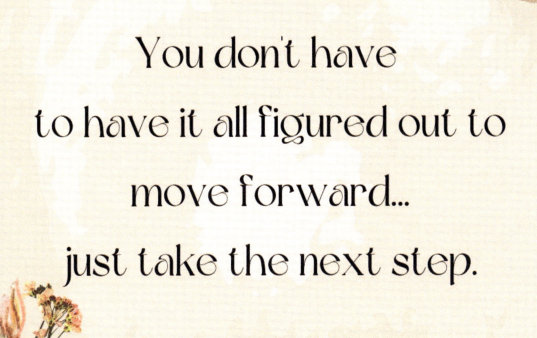

You don't have to have it all figured out to move forward... just take the next step.

LEARNING FROM MARGOT IN LIFE AND IN DEATH

January 31, 2021

For the last decade, one aspect of my life was as predictable as clockwork. If it was the second Monday of the month, you would find me at O'Charley's with my next-door neighbor Margot. We would be in a booth in the bar, over by the window, chatting with our favorite waitress, Brett, or "Sweetheart," as Margot called her. We'd be confirming that we wanted "the usual." And so, Brett-Sweetheart would put in our order for two glasses of wine each, to give us happy hour pricing, and then bring us the first one. She'd keep an eye out on us and bring the second glass when the first was gone.

Dinner rolls with lots of extra butter came out then too. Ultimately, we ordered dinner. By the end of three hours, all food and beverages consumed, we were ready to leave a big tip to thank Brett-Sweetheart for her warm hospitality, say our goodbyes, and promise to return soon. We all knew when. Like I said, clockwork!

Chai on Life

Similarly, if it was the last Monday of the month, you would find me at United Dairy Farmers eating ice cream with Margot. We always hoped for a repeat performance of the night our server was so disgruntled with her boss that she was planning to quit. To spite him, she was serving up extra-generous portions of ice cream and gave us enormous double scoops, an ice cream lover's dream come true. Suffice it to say that turnover was so high at UDF that we never knew our servers' real names, but to Margot, they were all "Sweetheart."

Though the drinking, dining, and ice cream were all delightful, the main wonderfulness of Margot was the fact that she was my motherhood mentor. She was eighteen years older than me, which made her children older than mine, which made her the one who showed me all the previews of coming attractions for my family.

Between us, we had eight kids and fifteen grandkids, so a lot to talk about. From the get-go, I told her all my problems with all my kids, but it took a couple years for her to confide as much in me. Hailing originally from New York, she had a tough outer shell. I see it now as an honor that she brought her rare complaints to me.

What was most helpful in these chats was Margot's "Poof-Poof

Philosophy." When our stories got too heavy or we found ourselves talking about situations over which we had no control, she would lift her hand overhead, wave it gently through the air, and say, "Poof-poof," blowing that topic away, or at least parking it somewhere until next time.

Travel was another thing Margot and I shared. We loved our trip to Mount Rushmore, Yellowstone, and the Grand Tetons, often choosing to have ice cream for lunch. Our Rocky Mountaineer trip through the Canadian Rockies was not as great. The tour company scheduled too much time for hiking! But *poof-poof*, we coped just fine. We whiled away the hours in the hotel bar doing our thing. We had plans for another vacation, this one to New Mexico, but COVID-19 postponed it, and before we could reschedule it, time ran out.

In May, Margot was diagnosed with lung cancer. Hopes for targeted therapies appeared but quickly vanished. By the start of August, she was in hospice care, and by the end of the month, she was gone.

In several visits during that time, I witnessed her decline from being Fully-Margot, to Not-Quite-Margot, to Not-Margot-At-All. It was a horrible progression. But, trail blazer until the end, she was imparting one more lesson for me and for my kids. She was teaching a new meaning to the concept of a biological clock and the non-*poof-poof*-able fact that it will run out.

As I get older and have more practice dealing with death, I would love to say that I have come to accept death, but that's not quite true. Instead, I have come to better understand the concept of dying. There is a brink from which we cannot return. To still be breathing is not the same as being alive. Those are the parts I accept.

As much as I loved Margot—and needed her in my life—it was time to let go when she reached that Not-Margot-At-All point. It was time to wish for the end without guilt.

It's hard to admit, but I did that. I wished for Margot's death. And when my time comes to follow in her footsteps, I hereby give my kids permission to follow in mine.

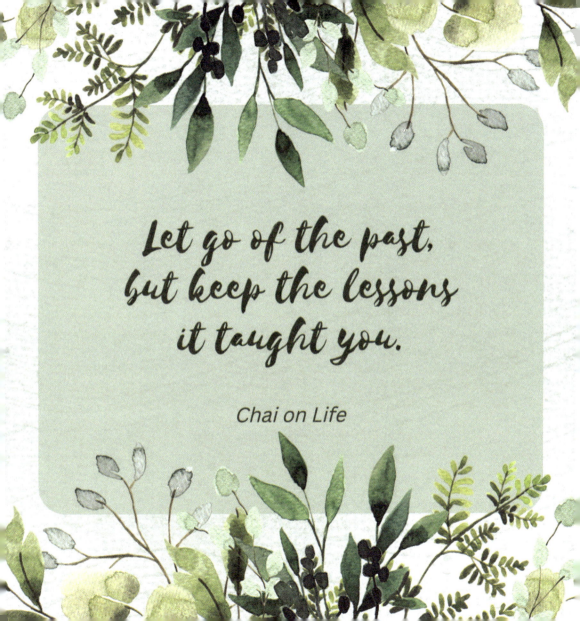

WORRYING ABOUT FIELD SOBRIETY TESTS AND OTHER ASPECTS OF AGING

January 24, 2022

Both my son and my ex-husband are tall. They are 6'4" and 6'3" respectively. Or at least they used to be. At a recent family gathering, we stood them back to back, only to find a large difference! Three or four inches! While it is true that my son is an amazing person in many ways, I don't think it's the case that he is growing taller at age 45. Super sleuth that I am, I'm thinking my 71-year-old ex has shrunk.

Frankly, this is shocking! As is the fact that I have such an old ex-husband! As is the fact that I will have a 70th birthday myself in a few weeks! Taken together, it seems like a good time to see how things *measure up* for me at this milestone.

- Taking this phrase literally

I sucked in my gut, threw back my shoulders, and pretended to have a string attached to the top of my head pulling me taller and taller as I allowed the nurse to measure me at my physician's office. All this effort proved that I am not measuring up; I am measuring down—I'm a full inch and a half shorter than in my prime.

Here's a troubling thought, though. Since my weight hasn't likewise decreased, proportionately speaking, I'm not as thin as I once was. This seriously messes with my self-image! (But thankfully, not so much with my BMI. Whew!)

- Manual dexterity

I congratulate my four-year-old grandson on his increasing manual dexterity—he can cut with scissors! As I do this, I notice changes in my ability as well. Pickle jar lids, the foil liner in my coffee creamer, a strand of hair on the floor: They all challenge me.

I remember a funny story about my dad when he was in his 80's. He took a jar of pickles back to the customer service desk at the grocery store to complain that he couldn't open it. I still laugh about it now, but I do so ruefully.

- Regarding wrinkles

I used to be able to relax my face so that the lines in my forehead went away. That's no longer in my skillset anymore.

- On the topic of vision

I am grateful that I can still see at a distance and thank God for reading glasses that help me see up close, but when I take my glasses off to wash my hair, how am I supposed to tell which bottle is the shampoo and which is the conditioner? Someone should tell hair care companies that I currently choose products based on the size of the font.

- I have another eye problem

I spent a lot of time wondering why the eyeliner I used for years was suddenly smudging daily, only to figure out that my eyelids droop, effectively blotting it off.

More rueful laughter is mine as I recall Meryl Streep in the movie *It's Complicated*. It sure used to be hilarious the way she manually held her eyelid up and explored cosmetic surgery, but not so much now.

- I also worry about field sobriety tests

HealthinAging.org tells me that 25 percent of all older adults—and 40 percent of those older than 75—have balance problems, and I admit to being among them. My friend Robin tells me to practice my balance by standing on one foot while I brush my teeth. Some days, this is not a pretty sight. It makes me wonder how I would fare if I ever had to do a field sobriety test.

Chai on Life

- On the topic of speed, but not vehicular

I have been walking an hour a day, five days a week, for more than 30 years. In the beginning, I'd walk four miles each day. I'm chagrinned to say that lately I walk a 19-minute mile, which equates to roughly three miles per hour.

Trying to put this in perspective, I think of the friend who described life's stages as the go-go years, the slow-go years, and the no-go years. On the one hand, I'm grateful I can still go…

- I have a two-pronged attitude problem to deal with

Regarding physical activity: For 13 years, I have worked out with a personal trainer. Then there are those 30 years of taking walks plus the little workout I'd do before going on one. Each day, I ask myself how long can I endure? Certainly, I won't be doing this when I'm 90. But how about 80? Or the soon-to-be-70?

Regarding my physical appearance: Back when I was 50, I told a favorite female doctor I thought it was time to give up waistbands in favor of muu-muus. She assured me it was not. She said the same thing when I was 55, 60, and 65, promising she would let me know when it was time. What happened next is that she retired without giving further instruction. Now what?

- Is it time to give up?

Clearly, it would be so easy to give up—both exercise and waistbands—and to admit defeat in the face of all these changes. But I don't plan on it. Why? Because borrowing from comedian Steven Wright, I don't want to be young when I die of old age. Thus, I will keep on keeping on for now, and revisit these topics in a year or 10 or 20. God willing…

Today's Goal

 Accept yourself

 Love yourself

 And keep moving forward

Can't Help
Loving that
Family of Mine

WE ARE FAMILY

December 10, 2019

Monday: My cousin Roz died. I got the news via text message while attending my grandson Josh's ninth birthday. When the party ended and I prepared to leave, I gave the news to the rest of the family, Josh included. He knows well what a first cousin is because he has seven of them, all of whom he adores. Hence, he could understand my sadness. He asked Rozie's age. I told him she was eleven years older than I am, which made us 67 and 78. I assured him that those ages might sound old but they really are not. He is a sweet and polite boy. He didn't argue with me but he was clearly skeptical.

Tuesday: I feel very fortunate that I live in Cincinnati, which is in driving distance of my hometown, St. Louis. It was therefore easy to travel the 373 miles to attend Rozie's funeral. I felt discombobulated as I drove. While Roz had struggled with mental illness her entire adult life, she was otherwise healthy. How could she have died? I felt guilty too. It had been a long time since I last visited her.

As I drove across the state line into Missouri, a sign said, "Welcome to St. Louis." At almost the same moment, my oldies radio station started to play

Chai on Life

"We Are Family." Suffice it to say this was an emotional "welcome home" for me.

Wednesday: At the funeral, Roz's nephew, Jimmy, performed the ceremony, sharing many personal and loving remarks. Roz's niece, Maggie, spoke too. These cousins had been among the superstars of Roz's caregiving team through the years. They could have told sad stories of bad days but they chose to remember the good times instead. Maggie's words were particularly eye-opening for me. She simply told of the things she and Roz loved doing together: shopping at Kohl's, listening to their favorite music, knitting, and watching Oprah's "Super Soul Sunday." Just mentioning these mundane activities made them glow with importance—they are the stuff of memories.

I felt sad that time had run out before I figured out a way to do more with Roz. Now I know. I, too, could have listened to Neil Diamond or Barbra Streisand with her. It could have been just that easy to figure out our togetherness.

In spite of my failure with Roz, I cherish family. I inherited this sentiment from my dad, whose one black cloud in life was the fact that beyond his parents and siblings, he had almost no family. Everyone else died in the Holocaust. This fact gives each of us born in the next generations a special significance. We're it. We're the family. Thus, after the funeral, I was delighted to have lunch with these loved ones at Cousin Jimmy's house.

The greatest thing about lunch was sharing tales of Roz and other relatives who are now gone. In retrospect, it doesn't really matter which stories we told, only that in telling the stories, our loved ones lived on. It delights me that there was an actual takeaway from the tales. Literally. We promised and then followed through on sending each other family recipes. Stuffed cabbage rolls! Mandel bread! "Moon" cookies!

The most difficult thing about the meal was realizing my exact place within the group. My paternal grandparents, my parents, and all my aunts and uncles on Dad's side of the family are gone. There were nine first cousins born into that group. With Roz, three of them now are deceased. Of the remaining, I am the fourth oldest. Age sixty-seven suddenly felt quite ancient. Perhaps I had protested too much that past Monday when chatting with grandson Josh.

After leaving Jimmy's house, I headed back to the cemetery where we had buried Roz. My parents are buried there too and I needed shoulders to cry on. I was saddened by Roz's death. I was disappointed in myself for not having been more involved with her during her lifetime. I was frightened by my own

Chai on Life

mortality. When I was able to calm myself, I made a promise to Mom and Dad that I would do a better job of staying in touch with the St. Louis family, with other relatives nationwide, and even with my kids and grandkids in Cincinnati.

Maggie's lesson tells me this is doable. Grand gestures are not always necessary. Small acts can suffice. I see a lot of emails and text messages in my future.

Rozie's gravesite is up at the front of the cemetery, so I passed it as I walked back to my car. Big clumps of earth filled her grave. The ground was in as much upheaval as I was. I know that in time, the earth will settle back down, as will my emotions. I hope and pray that, as this happens, I will keep my promise to my parents. This thought will certainly help: I am a family elder now and I have a responsibility to the clan. We need to stay close, because we're it. We're the family.

Each generation will reap
what the
former generation
has sown.

CANNED PINK SALMON, PRUNES, AND DRIED APRICOTS

January 27, 2020

There was no Walgreens advertising section in my Sunday newspaper today. This gave me pause, not because I love shopping at Walgreens, but because my parents did and my beloved Aunt Tillie did, and because every time I see this particular newspaper insert, I think of them… fondly.

Their love of the store boiled down to this: They always wanted to buy canned pink salmon, prunes, and dried apricots at a good price.

My Jewish heritage tells me that the deceased live on in the acts of loving kindness they performed. And this is true! But they also live on in hundreds of little ways.

I am grateful that something so simple as a Walgreens ad can bring back such fond memories of such beloved people.

OF MATZAH BALLS, LEGOS, AND VARIOUS THINGS IN BETWEEN

October 7, 2019

I hosted a big holiday dinner at my house the other evening in celebration of Rosh Hashana, the Jewish New Year. Afterward, as I sat digesting the meal and the experience, these thoughts occurred to me…

Regarding matzah balls: We've all heard of turning lemons into lemonade, but this year I turned illness into matzah ball soup instead. In May, I experienced a frightening medical "event" that sent me to the emergency room twice and included an overnight hospital admission. Five weeks later, every scary diagnosis was ruled out and it was determined that my event was a fluke—thank God—but that five-week waiting period was scary.

As my kids gathered around in support, my daughter Lisa made me a pot of matzah ball soup. It was delicious. And it was just the elixir I needed. And it got me thinking…one of the most difficult things for me to do at the various Jewish holidays is to make the matzah ball soup. Here was a solution to

Chai on Life

my problem—a new soup chef! It's mind-boggling that this truly huge holiday gift came to me right there in the midst of my medical misery.

Regarding mashed potatoes and other side dishes: When I think of preparing a Jewish holiday meal, one main image comes to mind—huge cauldrons of boiling water. Such pots are needed to prepare four things on my menu: gefilte fish, mashed potatoes, chicken stock, and matzah balls. The logistics of what-cooks-when—plus the washing of all those pots—have been daunting. Having given away the broth and the balls to Lisa, I turned to my other daughter, Shana, to handle the potatoes. That left me with one very manageable pot, and an indescribable sense of relief. It is said that insanity is doing the same thing over and over again expecting different results. This year we did things differently.

As is always the case, my other guests offered to bring things for our meal, and this time I took them up on it. Hence, salad, hot veggies, kugel, homemade challah, and bottles of sparkling cider made it to our table without my involvement. This help allowed me to focus on entrées and desserts, which were as manageable as that one pot of boiling water.

As we all sat down to enjoy the meal together, I was aware and grateful that this year's holiday experience was emotionally filling as opposed to physically draining.

Regarding Bundt pans: This may very well be a reflection on my lack of baking skills, but I often have a helluva time removing a Bundt cake from a Bundt pan. As much as I grease and flour the pan in advance, there seems to be no guarantee the cake will actually come out of it—in one piece—after baking. For Rosh Hashana this year, my cake fell out of the pan with ease, sending me directly from the kitchen to my bedroom to record the joyous occurrence in my gratitude journal. I could take some credit here and report that I recently threw out my Bundt pan from 1973 and got a new one. Perhaps it has a magical new finish, or maybe I just got lucky. No matter. The lesson of the Bundt pan is gratitude.

Regarding Lego Duplo blocks: Though everyone helped wash dishes, clean up after the meal, and even return folding chairs to the basement, there was one mess that somehow got left behind—Lego Duplo blocks were all over the living room floor. Duplo blocks are the big, chunky Legos intended for toddlers, and they are part of the toy collection I keep at my house. All of my grandchildren—now ages 2, 6, 6, 6, 6, 8, 9, 11, 11, and 13—have played with these blocks through the years.

Most memorable was the way little Leo (now 9) would knock down every tower I built. In return, I'd scoop him up and torture him with kisses as he laughed in delight. Recently, my 8-year-old grandson and his 6-year-old brother asked me to buy regular Legos, which I did, though this very tangible sign of the kids growing up made me ache. Thus, when Duplo blocks remained on the floor after the last guest departed, I left them there for a couple of days, cherishing my memories.

Cherishing memories? Yes, I've always liked to do that. When I was a child, my family belonged to a group called the Willick Family Circle. It was composed of my maternal grandfather's eight siblings and their families. There was even a recording secretary for the group, and my mom was it. I loved reading through the green notebook she kept. It contained her minutes recalling all the good times. I especially loved that each report closed the same way: "And a good time was had by all."

Regarding our Rosh Hashana dinner in 2019—I think the same benediction applies.

And I am as grateful for that as I am for the miracle of the Bundt pan.

INFLUENCERS ARE EVERYWHERE, NOT JUST ON SOCIAL MEDIA

January 14, 2020

Do you remember the comic strip *Cathy*? It was drawn by Cathy Guisewite and ran in newspapers from 1976-2010.

The mother/daughter relationship was a frequent topic in *Cathy*, and my favorite cartoonist punchline from it is this: "Funny how much better we understand the Jell-O when we've seen the mold." Of course, we are molded by more than just our mothers, so today I remember six people who influenced the person I am today.

Rose Kleiner was my mom. She was very effective in the world. She got things done. She ran our four-person household with ease. Even a winter day with frozen pipes in the kitchen did not faze her. She cooked dinner as usual, but washed dishes in the bathroom. She let stresses like frozen pipes "roll off her back."

Her most often stated beliefs were that "it's always something," and that in life there was "never a dull moment." Mom and I sometimes butted heads because I took an emotional slant on all issues while she took a practical one. I am beginning to see that as the main-momma for my kids and grandkids, strength is a good image to project.

Morrie Kleiner was my dad. He was a marshmallow of a man, famous for the "love squeezes" he gave his grandkids. He was a hugger, not a fighter, and his sweetness was loved by all. Dad had a blood disorder that caused him to need transfusions regularly. When the problem started, those transfusions occurred every few months. Towards the end of his life, they were every couple of weeks. Picc lines, visiting nurses, blood draws, etc. were then a big part of his life, yet he never complained. Instead, he said, "Everyone has something. This is mine."

I tend to smoosh their philosophies together to come up with my own. Not only is it always something, but if it weren't this, it would be something else, so deal with the situation at hand, and be happy it's not something worse.

Mary Willick was my maternal grandmother. That one time I ran away from home at age six, I went to her house, exactly one mile away. From elementary school through my first job as a college graduate, I often went to her house for lunch—a plateful of potato latkes and milk served in a coffee cup. I adored the woman. She was the one I turned to when I dropped out of that too-far-away-from-home first college. I was afraid of what everyone would say. *Her advice?* Take what others say "to foot." What she meant: Listen to them politely, and then walk away.

Auntillie was my dad's sister. She was a people person extraordinaire. They say there are only six degrees of separation between individuals, but that wasn't true for Auntillie. She not only knew everyone, but she stayed in touch with everyone. In my mind's eye, she is sitting at her kitchen table, hands poised above her Royal typewriter, composing letters to out-of-town loved ones.

I once asked her how to stay in touch with a relative who was a pain in the rear. This person never called me, yet when I called her, I couldn't get off the phone. Did I really need to hear—in detail—about this relative's hairdresser's sister-in-law? Auntillie told me it was indeed important to call that relative! Just not very often.

It is validating to note that both of these family members—women who were greatly loved and admired—had a game plan for difficult people.

Chai on Life

Smooshing their philosophies together, I allow myself to walk away when necessary, while never walking completely out of range.

Sylvia Eckert was my mother-in-law. OK, so we didn't always get along, but I think of her often because of that day, long ago, when I was newly married to her son. She stopped by my house to ask if I wanted to join her and my father-in-law at the deli for lunch. I turned her down! My plan for the afternoon was to wash the kitchen floor! She calmly explained that the kitchen floor would always be there to wash, while an invitation to do something fun was not always available. I liked that philosophy, and the bagel, cream cheese, and lox I ate that day.

My grandpa, Sam Willick, was another purveyor of joy. Grandma and Grandpa's duplex was only four or five houses away from the corner market, which had a counter full of penny candies. After Friday night dinners at their house, Grandpa would reach into his pocket and pull out what seemed like a HUGE handful of change. My cousins, brother, and I were allowed to take it all, and spend it all, and eat all that candy…as long as we also bought the evening newspaper for Grandpa.

Both stories are wonderful reminders to find the JOY in the JOurneY.

It is said that you become who you hang out with, and indeed, these people have molded the person I am today. Dealing with life. Dealing with others. Recognizing and appreciating the joy in each day. I am proud to live by their example.

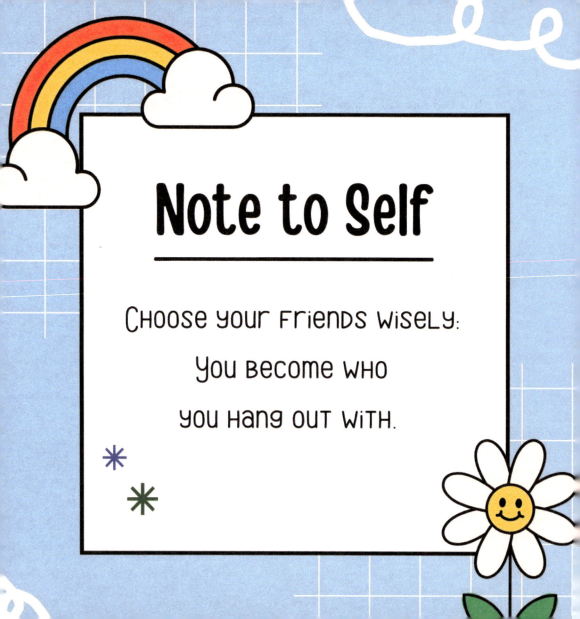

UPON TURNING SEVENTY

February 12, 2022

Dear sixteen-year-old Lorie,

You've been listening repeatedly to Simon and Garfunkel's new album *Bookends*. Indeed, you know all the words. While the nation laughs along with the "coo, coo, ca-choo" of "Mrs. Robinson," you instead are haunted by the lyrics of the song "Old Friends." Something reverberates in you as they sing, "How terribly strange to be seventy."

You will be amazed how suddenly fifty-four years will pass and you will arrive at that strange age. That's where I find myself today. As I look to the past and to the future, I have a few things to tell you. First, previews of coming attractions. Next, three tips for handling it all.

This is your life:

I know you, girlfriend. All you want is to be a mom. Indeed, you often chat with God, "If You can just let me know that at some point I will have kids, I can relax and enjoy my life."

Chai on Life

I also know you hate school, but you are a good student. Therefore, you feel compelled to go to college. You will do that. You will get a degree in education. Your rationale is this: On the off-chance your someday husband should die young, you will have something to fall back on. You do not plan to have a career, though. Never, ever.

And then you will get married! And have three amazing kids!

But then you will get divorced, which was not in the plan.

And then you will have a career! I know this is a ridiculous outcome for a born-to-be homemaker, but it is true nonetheless.

Twenty-eight years and ten grandchildren later, you will stand where I stand today. You will be seventy-years-old and proud of yourself for handling all the unexpected twists and turns in life. Three philosophies will get you to this stage.

The wise words of Mom and Dad:

Mom had two common rejoinders to life: "never a dull moment," and/or "it's always something." The boring nature of these comments belie the multitude of horrible life experiences they covered over. They remind us not to get too excited no matter how terrible the moment.

Then there was Dad. You'll see that in later life, he had a blood disorder which required transfusions galore over a dozen years. He never complained. Instead, he said, "Everyone has something. This is mine."

My extrapolation is this: If you didn't have whatever problem you have, you'd have a different one. So calmly accept the one you've got. On a daily basis, you're learning how to deal with your never-dull moments. Keep it up!

Meanwhile, an old prayer from Rosh Hashana will help you understand life's problems.

This prayer/poem was written by Rabbi Alvin Fine. It will reverberate in your soul as much as the Simon and Garfunkel lyrics. It begins this way:

"Birth is a beginning

And death a destination,

And life is a journey…"

One of the stages of the journey is that we go from "defeat to defeat to defeat" until we finally learn that they don't really matter. Victory lies solely

Chai on Life

in making the journey. We have to keep on keeping on.

And this song will set you on the right kind of path:

Mom and Dad loved this song which means you will too. Their cantor sang it to Mom during a hospital visit when she was dying. After that, Dad couldn't say the name of the song without a catch in his voice. You will feel the same way. But beyond that, the song lyrics will speak to you. Written by Debbie Friedman, the song is called *Mi Shebeirach*. It is a prayer for healing and renewal, and it contains this enlightening line: "Help us find the courage to make our lives a blessing."

Thus, we are reminded that the journey has to be meaningful, honorable, and worthy of our best selves. We have to use our talents to make a contribution to the world in some way large or small.

And oh yes, as surely as Dad was wise in reminding us, we will all have problems, so is it important to know that we all have talents. One of yours is the *courage* to live this kind of life.

OK then, here's what you need to do:

Now that you know all of this, Little Lor, do what you promise in your chats with God: Relax and enjoy life! And I, at the terribly strange age of seventy, will try to do the same.

XO,

Big Lor

The G Words: Gratitude and God

30 REASONS TO BE GRATEFUL AT MY GRANDDAUGHTER'S SOCCER GAME

September 27, 2021

Let's just say it out loud: I am not a confident driver or parker. So, when I survived a recent parking challenge, I was so overcome with gratitude that it colored every thought in my head. Here, then, are the 30 thoughts in my head:

1. I am grateful for having the courage to try to find a parking space at the elementary school where my eight-year-old granddaughter was playing her first soccer game of the season. The once spacious lot is now ravaged by construction as additions to the building are being made. This has turned parking into a stress test.

2. I am grateful for making it around that very tight curve where some extremely unthoughtful and unkind person left their car even though it blocked the flow of traffic for everyone else.

3. I am grateful that on the other side of that blockade, I found a parking space because I wasn't running the gauntlet again. I was just going to go home!

Chai on Life

4. I am grateful for knowing that I should take a few deep breaths to calm down when I am stressed.

5. I am grateful for continuing to do the deep breathing until it worked and reminded me…

6. I am grateful that this school district has enough money to do extensive renovations even if it impairs parking.

7. And while we're on the topic, I'm grateful to live in a school district that often ranks high on various state and national lists.

8. And stepping back a bit further, I'm grateful that all my kids live in Cincinnati, and that all my grandkids have the good fortune of attending schools in this fine school district.

9. I am grateful for being on good terms with my kids so that I'm given the team schedule and welcome to show up for games.

10. I am grateful that I get along with my ex-husband, the Gramps of the group, because he might show up too.

11. As I get out of my car, I am grateful that even though the soccer fields are in upheaval and not well-marked, my son-in-law, the coach, is tall enough to see, and so I know where to go.

12. I'm grateful for knowing exactly where to go because the weather app tells me it's 85 degrees outside and feels like 97. Wandering in the desert might have worked for Moses, but it doesn't work for me.

13. I'm grateful to have good enough knees, hips, and back to make it all the way over to the soccer field while schlepping a lawn chair.

14. Darn! I left the sun umbrella and water bottle in the car, but I am extremely grateful for what I've got—a hair elastic in the bottom of my purse that will allow me to pull my hair back!

15. I'm grateful to see my granddaughter, my "Cookie," out there on the field, and grateful that she sees me too. (Perhaps this will buy me an extra visit at the nursing home when she and I are a lot older.)

16. Seeing my son-in-law on the field, I am grateful that he is an involved dad. He has coached soccer teams for all three of his daughters—my grandgirls.

17. Seeing somebody else's grandma on the sidelines with her shirt on inside-out, I am grateful it's not me.

18. Back to that handsome son-in-law, I'm grateful that he has a job that allows him the flexibility to be a coach.

19. I'm grateful that he and the girls—and indeed all my kids and grand kids—have the good health to participate in extracurricular activities.

20. I'm grateful that my children and children-in-law work so hard to give their kids myriad opportunities like this.

21. Wait! Look what I see! My daughter—Cookie's mom—is walking toward us! She is the #1 spectator I hoped would appear! I am grateful to see her—and the sun umbrella she is carrying.

Chai on Life

22. I am grateful that I am the only grandparent in attendance, so I won't have to share her with anyone.

23. I'm grateful to have the rest of the game to chat with her and to catch up on all the news that she might otherwise be too busy to tell me.

24. I'm grateful that none of the little red-faced soccer players passed out in the August heat. I promised my daughter that Cookie would be fine, and I'm always gladdened to deliver on a promise.

25. I'm grateful that our team scored a couple of times, and grateful to understand that it doesn't matter if you win or lose; it's how you play the game.

26. I'm grateful for walking back to the car with my son-in-law and getting to hear the family news from his point of view.

27. I'm very grateful for getting back to my dependable car with dependable air conditioning that took me home to my likewise dependably air-conditioned home…

28. Where with immense gratitude, I guzzled lots of ice-cold water.

29. Feeling better now, I'm grateful that I was able to delete the expletive in talking about that person in item #2 above.

30. And I am grateful that I'm able to see the bright side. Yes, I am a wimp about finding parking places, but look how strong I am in finding gratitude!

LONG-STORY-LISTENER
April 10, 2018

"Long story short" is a common expression these days. The speaker uses it to shorten a SAGA into a SNIPPET. But what if you need to tell the whole long story? For that you need a Long-Story-Listener. That's what my friend Robin is for me.

Robin and I have many things in common.

- We both have three adult children.

- We are both Jewish and go to the same temple.

- Both of us have served as President of the Temple's Sisterhood.

- We are both liberal in our politics, in favor of every social service issue that appears on the ballot.

- We both have a love of mankind, but both find it difficult to deal with people.

Chai on Life

- We love to read and are in a book club together.

- We love to go to the movies.

- We love dissecting all the tales we read and see.

- She cries over these stories in darkened theaters and at home; I cry in those places and in public, sometimes to her dismay.

- She has taught me to love sitting at a bar to have a drink and dinner. She's a straight-up martini with olives girl, while I take my margarita with any tequila as long as the bartender uses a lot of it. And isn't it great that she is still capable of driving after one drink?

- We both love to eat, though she's more of a foodie than I am. (But, when I need to go slumming—to White Castle or to a Skyline Chili Parlor— she loans me her husband, Van, who likewise loves junk food.)

- And of course, we both worry about every morsel we eat and how it will affect the bathroom scale come morning.

Though all of these things bond our friendship, we have one secret ingredient that brings us super closeness—we are walking partners, so we spend scads of time together. We aim to walk five days a week, for an hour each day, traveling about 2 ½ miles daily. Allowing for vacations and inclement weather,

I will assume an 80 percent rate of reaching our target. By this calculation, we walk 200 days and travel 500 miles each and every year.

Better than all the calories burned in this exercise is the fact that those 200 days represent 200 hours of conversation. I am willing to bet there are some husbands and wives who don't talk to each other that much in a year, especially considering those who are addicted to their cell phones. Be that as it may, this amount of time allows us to tell each other our complex life experiences in minute detail, something we would never take the time to do in a telephone call or in an email. And of course, we could never do it in a TXT MSG. KWIM?

Love her as I do, I am soon to be broken hearted because Robin is moving away. Remember those three adult kids of hers? Well, they live in Boston, Providence, and Brooklyn, while she and Van find themselves too many miles away in Ohio. Their home, one block away from mine, is on the market. And it's waiting for the purchase contract that will change their lives and mine.

A mutual friend tells us that we can still walk and talk together via the cell phone, and I sure hope this becomes our reality. While I have many wonderful friends in whom I confide, Robin is the record holder, and I will miss her. Clearly that's an understatement, but I won't elaborate because she's uncomfortable when I cry in public.

Life lesson for one and all: If you have a long-story-listener in your life, recognize that person as the wonderful, amazing, astounding friend (and gift!) that they are and be grateful for every day you share!

FROM GOD'S LIPS TO MY EARS

May 19, 2022

Yesterday, I said this to my writing friend: "I hope a literary agent finds one of my online stories and **COMES TO ME** to suggest a compilation of my vignettes for a book!

My friend responded: "From your lips to God's ears!"

We both chuckled.

This morning, as I was writing my "morning pages" as suggested in *The Artist's Way: A Spiritual Path to Higher Creativity*, I'm supposed to "vent" in my journal for three pages. Since I didn't have much to vent about, I copied the list of twenty creative affirmations author Julia Cameron includes. When I got to my favorite one, "I am willing to let God create through me," I chuckled again.

Thanks to Cameron's journaling technique—which causes creative ideas to flourish—perhaps my friend's words were directionally challenged, and

Chai on Life

THIS is the correct phraseology:

From God's lips to my ears!

I'm ready to listen…

Remember: "Listen" and "silent" contain the same letters.

GOD DANCING ON THE CEILING
June 25, 2019

My house is built on a man-made lake. Every window in the back has a beautiful view of the water. Yet, the most stunning thing about the lake is that the morning sun bounces off it, sending ripples of light through my mini-blinds and onto my ceiling. I like to think of this as God dancing there.

This thought came to me during the first days of living in the house. I was a soon-to-be-divorced woman who was in many ways scared to death of the future. As I lay in bed on one of those mornings, three bands of light from the three windows in the room danced away. As I puzzled over what they were trying to tell me, these words popped into my head: "You are not alone. I am with you. Fear not."

These words soothed my soul.

I have lived in the house over twenty years now and of course I have become very comfortable with my life, divorce included. But a residue of that time sticks with me, namely the thought—perhaps belief—that God dances on my ceiling each sunny morning.

I never thought I was teaching anyone anything, but as I started to have grandchildren and they started to visit my house, I showed them my ceiling. Though my three children were raised in the Jewish faith, my grandchildren are being raised in various manners of believing in God—or not. Hence, it was interesting to hear from one of the little kids that he believes in God… when he's at my house. Perhaps it's because of the very tangible dance routine we see.

Lucky gal that I am, all my kids and grandkids live within a five-mile radius of my house. Our Monday routine is that any child who is not in school full time—or who has a day off from school—comes to my house for a nursery-school-like day that we call Marmel School—"Marmel" is my grandma name. When the parents bring the kids over for the day, they often come in with coffee.

Thus it was that my son, a former school teacher, was with his kids one morning at my house. As the light show began on the ceiling, he took the opportunity to do a science lesson. "Do you know why that light is sparkling on the ceiling?" he asked. The kids shouted in unison, "It's God dancing on the ceiling!" The science lesson ended there.

Throughout the years of Marmel School, all the little kids have delighted in this phenomenon. Sometimes the light show is more dramatic than other times and the kids excitedly shout to come into this room or that to see God. One day, the light show was rather lethargic and we had to search from room to room to find God. But there He/She was, finally, in a little area on my bedroom wall. My grandson was four years old at the time when he said, "Look, Marmel, God's a transformer! He's on the wall instead of the ceiling!"

Recently, I had a scary health "episode" which caused me to spend hours in the emergency room followed by a night in the hospital. When I was released and came home, I was not at all confident about my health, or more to the point, what number of days were being left to me. As I woke up that first morning at home, I was actively aware—and grateful—that I had woken up, and as I lay there saying a little prayer of thanks, I noticed God up there on my ceiling. "Oh, wow," I thought. "My old friend's here to comfort me."

It's now a couple weeks since the last hospitalization. And life goes on, thank God. Thus, a much-needed repair to my home is in progress—I am getting new windows. It was only as the installers ripped the old windows out

Chai on Life

on the back of the house that I started to worry about how this might impact…well, God in my life. Truth be told, I have never understood the science behind the phenomenon, and the lesson my son was beginning to give was thwarted by divine intervention.

So, would new windows change things? They are treated in such a way that UV rays don't get in, but is God likewise blocked? This question plagued me through several rainy mornings. But finally, there was a sunny day. What happened? Proof positive that God was still with me! Whew!

I know some will scoff at this story. They will say that the concept of God is just a crutch for those not strong enough to face the world alone. In part, I agree with them. That is exactly what I have confessed to here, especially on those days when my spirit is limping.

But let's not forget the wise words of my grandson: "God is a trans-former." So on other days—those days when my spirit is dancing—God is both light and delight.

I am grateful.

P. S.

Here's the whole book in short form
for those with too little time to read. KWIM?

- Your mind believes what you tell it, so tell it positive things.
- Be You! You're BE-YOU-tiful just the way you are.
- There are lots of ways to say I LOVE YOU.
- You are brave and brilliant and oh so resilient.
- Flawsome: A person who embraces their "flaws" and knows they are awesome regardless.
- Praise, like sunlight, helps all things grow.
- The secret to your success is found in your daily routine.
- A little bit + a little bit = a whole lot.
- Blessed are the flexible because they will not be bent out of shape.
- If it ain't broke, don't fix it.
- Life teaches you a new lesson every day if you are attentive enough to listen.

Chai on Life

- You can't go back and change the beginning, but you can start where you are and change the ending.
- On the road to success, even the smallest steps move you forward.
- The secret to having it all is knowing you already do.
- Life isn't about waiting for the storm to pass. It's about learning to dance in the rain.
- Sometimes sitting and doing nothing is the best thing you can do.
- Good friends help you find important things when you have lost them: your smile, your hope, and your courage.
- Every day is a new opportunity to become a better version of yourself.
- Selfcare: the radical notion that you deserve your own attention.
- AND
- You owe yourself the love you so freely give to other people.
- AND
- What if you simply devoted this week to loving yourself?
- Forgive unto others as you would have them forgive unto you.
- Sometimes asking for help is the bravest move you can make. You don't have to go it alone.
- Be strong enough to stand alone, smart enough to know when you need help, and brave enough to ask for it.
- When your heart speaks, take good notes.

- Choose life and live it.
- Remember the past. Create the present. Inspire the future.
- You don't have to have it all figured out to move forward…Just take the next step.
- Let go of the past, but keep the lessons it taught you.
- Accept yourself, love yourself, and keep moving forward.
- Each generation will reap what the former generation has sown.
- Memory is a way of holding onto things you love.
- Today's little moments become tomorrow's precious memories.
- Choose your friends wisely: You become who you hang out with.
- Relax…and find the JOY in the JOurneY
- There is always something to be grateful for.
- A good friend is like a four-leaf clover—hard to find and lucky to have.
- Remember: "Listen" and "silent" contain the same letters.
- If you can't believe in God, believe in sunbeams. Either way, bask in the warmth.

ABOUT THE AUTHOR

Lorie Kleiner Eckert is a dynamic author whose passion for words spans various mediums. With four published books and two blogs, she shares personal stories aimed at inspiring others. Her latest book, "*Love Loss and Moving On,*" creatively intertwines memoir, unauthorized biography, and flights of fancy as she navigates her journey through loss using a crush on British actor Bill Nighy as a catalyst for healing. Her previous work, "*I Need a Man's Pants to Wash,*" includes essays on being a single woman in mid-life. Her earlier books, "*Get Quiet and Listen,*" and "*With This Ring I Journey,*" blend personal anecdotes with her unique quilt designs, symbolizing her multifaceted storytelling approach.

Beyond her written endeavors, Lorie is also a captivating motivational speaker. From 1994 to 2004, she addressed over 22,000 people across 11 states, combining her inspirational words with a visual showcase of her quilts. Her talks, which range from self-acceptance to embracing life's journeys, are imbued with the same warmth and wisdom found in her writing. This dual approach of spoken and quilted words underscores her belief in the power of storytelling to teach and inspire.

A proud mother of three and grandmother of ten, Lorie currently resides in Cincinnati. Her life's journey has taken her from St. Louis to San Diego and Los Angeles, enriching her perspective and creative output. Whether through her Etsy shop showcasing her fiber art or her engaging social media presence, Lorie continues to spread her message of positivity and resilience, encouraging others to find and embrace their own stories.

A NOTE IN CLOSING:

I hope reading *Chai on Life* will inspire you to follow in my footsteps and to write down the stories of your life.

Since getting started is the hard part, why not use the book itself as a jumping off point? For instance, the Prologue is summarized with this lesson:

Your mind believes what you tell it, so tell it positive things.

Perhaps this statement alone evokes something in you. If so, grab a spiral notebook and write down what you are thinking! If not, here are three prompts to write about instead. (Write about one of them or all of them. There is no right or wrong, just what feels best to you.)

- Make a list of 5 to 10 positive things about yourself.
- Make a list of 5 to 10 things your friends would say are positive about you.
- Make a list of the friends who help you to be most positive in life.

That was easy, right? And hopefully enlightening.

For more writing prompts, visit the home page of my website, **LorieKleinerEckert.com**, where I will post new prompts weekly.

JOT DOWN A THOUGHT OR TWO NOW...